# JOB SEARCH LETTERS THAT GET RESULTS

## Books by Drs. Ron and Caryl Krannich

# JOB SEARCH LETTERS THAT GET RESULTS

Ronald L. Krannich, Ph.D.
Caryl Rae Krannich, Ph.D.

IMPACT PUBLICATIONS
Manassas Park, VA

# JOB SEARCH LETTERS THAT GET RESULTS:
## 201 Great Examples!

**Library of Congress Cataloguing-in-Publication Data**

Krannich, Ronald L.
    Job Search Letters That Get Results / Ronald L. Krannich, Caryl Rae Krannich.
        p.   cm.
     ISBN 0-942710-70-3 : $12.95.
     1. Resumes (Employment) 2. Job hunting. I. Krannich, Caryl Rae.
II. Title.
HF5383.K714   1992
808'.06665—dc20                       92-18655
                                     CIP

For information on distribution or quantity discount rates, Tel. 703/361-7300, Fax 703/335-9486, or write to: Sales Department, IMPACT PUBLICATIONS, 9104-N Manassas Drive, Manassas Park, VA 22111. Distributed to the trade by National Book Network, 4720 Boston Way, Suite A, Lanham, MD 20706, Tel. 301/459-8696.

# CONTENTS

# PREFACE

Finding a job is all about communicating your qualifications to potential employers. You do this through numerous mediums and channels, from letters and resumes to telephone and face-to-face interviews. Your ultimate goal is to get a job interview that hopefully turns into a rewarding job you both do well and enjoy doing.

But communicating your qualifications to potential employers is easier said than done. After all, you are often dealing with strangers who know little or nothing about you as either a person or a professional. Furthermore, most people are not used to writing resumes and letters nor initiating contacts with strangers. If you are like many other job seekers, you would rather be doing something else with your time than trying to get employers to take notice of your qualifications and invite you to interviews.

Like giving a speech before a group, writing letters to strangers is one of those tasks many people prefer avoiding. It's more than just work. For some, it's filled with anxiety. For others, it's simply difficult to do—they don't know what to say or how to say it.

This book is designed to take the anxiety out of writing job search letters. If followed carefully, it should result in moving your job search into the direction of more job interviews.

The 201 job search letters presented in the following pages are written for a variety of job search situations. Taken together, they represent an important compendium of job search communication. Examined individually, they are addressed to specific situations requiring some form of written communication. Each letter is structured around two job search considerations:

- the job search process—from skills identification to conducting research, networking, interviewing, and accepting an offer.

- principles of effective job search communication and writing.

Career counselors will find many of these letters fit perfectly into their job search and career planning approaches. Job seekers will find these examples answer many of their questions concerning *"what to do," "what to say," "how to say it,"* and *"what to do next."* In contrast to other books on job search letters, this one pulls together a large variety of job search communication that represents important actions you should take at various stages of your job search. As such, it is more than just another job search letter example book. It represents some of the most important communication that should take place in any job search. For example, in the following pages you will find letters to

- start as well as stop your job search

- develop contacts and uncover job leads

- broadcast your qualifications to potential employers

- follow-up on earlier communication

- develop good relations with a new employer

You'll see how important it is to clearly communicate your purpose, energy, enthusiasm, intelligence, and likability in these letters—important qualities sought by employers in job interviews but which are difficult to express in the format of a resume. You will learn that the simple social grace of writing a brief thank you letter can make a real difference in how you are perceived by an employer, regardless of the quality of your cover letter and resume. You will learn why many of your letters must include a follow-up statement—a critical element missing in most examples of job search letters.

Overall, our examples represent the richness and texture—as well as the complexities, challenges, and frustrations—found in most job searches. What emerges from these letters are some of the basic realities involved in finding a job.

Whatever you do, make sure your job search letters represent the "unique you." The temptation, of course, is to creatively plagiarize others' examples rather than produce your own job search letters from scratch. We strongly recommend that you avoid the pitfalls of simply copying someone else's letter—no matter how good. For how you write your letters and express your own interests, personality, and drive will say a lot about how you will handle yourself on the job. Creatively plagiarizing letters produced by others may indicate how you plan to do the job—cutting corners rather than fully using your abilities and skills. Use our letters as departure points for identifying the types of letters you need to write and what you need to include in your letters, especially the importance of follow-up statements and expressions of purpose, energy, enthusiasm, intelligence, and likability—qualities employers want to hire in addition to your experience and qualifications. Except in the face-to-face interview, there is no better way of expressing these qualities than in the form of job search letters.

Please be forwarned that most of the names and addresses in our examples are fictitious. If you attempt to send letters to these names and addresses, your mail will most likely be returned with the appropriate notation—"Address Unknown."

We wish you well in your job search. Finding a job is often a tough and disappointing road to travel. But with the help of these 201 examples of effective job search communication, you should be able to give your job search renewed direction as you clearly communicate your qualifications—and other important qualities—to employers. In the end, you will get results if you avoid the pitfalls and follow the basic principles outlined in Chapter Two and expressed in our examples.

# JOB SEARCH LETTERS THAT GET RESULTS

## Chapter One

# WRITE YOUR WAY TO CAREER SUCCESS

Are you an effective writer when it comes to writing letters important to your career? Do you regularly write letters that command the attention of employers who call you for job interviews? Do you routinely send thank you letters to individuals who assisted you or invited you to interviews? Are you a thoughtful person who makes a habit of communicating your personal and professional values to others in writing? Is the content of your letters employer-centered rather than self-centered? Do you mention benefits to others rather than benefits to yourself? Do your letters have sufficient impact to move others to take actions that benefit you?

If you answer "no" or "maybe" to any of these questions, then this book is for you. It will show you how to **get results** from your job search letters.

## WRITING RIGHT

Most job hunters are primarily concerned with writing good resumes and conducting effective interviews. Few see writing activities beyond the resume as important to their job search. However, it is increasingly clear that writing job search letters plays a critical role in conducting an effective job search. In fact, some employers report a well-crafted cover letter or a thoughtful thank you letter is sometimes more important to getting the job than the resume or interview.

Individuals who write powerful letters also are those who tend to write excellent resumes and conduct effective job interviews. They have a clear understanding of the role of letter writing in the overall job search process. They view letter writing as an essential ingredient in their efforts to persuade others to do things they ordinarily would not do—invite them to an interview as well as offer them the job. Going beyond just writing attractive letters, they produce excellent form and content that clearly communicate their qualifications to employers. Above all, they know how to write, produce, distribute, and follow-up their letters with maximum impact.

That is our task in the following pages—make sure you become an effective job seeker who can write right and thus write your way to job search success. We'll outline key letter writing, production, distribution, and follow-up principles as well as provide you with 201 examples of letters to be used for numerous job search occasions. These examples illustrate the key principles in writing right for job search success.

## JOB SEARCH LETTERS

A job search letter is any letter designed to promote the process of finding a job and thereby enhance your career visibility and acceptance to others. An effective job search letter is one that gets read and responded to in positive ways. These letters get the attention of readers who remember you, refer you to others, or contact you for further information or invite you to a job interview.

> *An effective job search letter is one that gets read and responded to in positive ways.*

As illustrated on page 3, job search letters are normally written during each phase of the job search. These letters should also be written while on the job. They not only help you find a job, they also help you keep your job as well as develop long-term professional and personal relations that define your network of relationships.

Job search letters may become the most important letters you will ever write. Their central purpose is to get others to take actions that will promote your career goals. They also have several other purposes:

- **Gather information for your reference and decision-making.** During each stage of you job search, you need important information for making additional decisions. Above all, you need to learn about the shape and direction of the job market. You should know about

## LETTERS IN THE JOB SEARCH

| PHASE | PROCESS | LETTERS |
|-------|---------|---------|
| 1 | Assess your abilities, skills, and interests | Inquiry for assessment services |
| 2 | State an objective | None |
| 3 | Conduct research | Information gathering letters on organizations, employers, and employment services. Approach letters to individuals. |
| 4 | Write resume and letters | Cover and resume letters |
| 5 | Network for information, advice, and referrals. | Approach, thank you, and follow-up letters |
| 6 | Conduct job interviews. | Thank you and follow-up letters |
| 7 | Negotiate the job offer. | Thank you letter |

specific jobs that interest you. You want to gather as much information about specific employers and organizations as possible. You do this by making telephone calls, meeting with individuals, and writing letters for information.

- **Communicate your major qualifications to employers.** These letters come in two forms: cover letters and resume letters. A cover letter accompanies a resume. As the name suggests, it provides cover for the resume. It is designed to grab the attention of the reader who, in turn, reviews the resume in depth. Resume letters substitute for resumes. They are written on occasions when it is more appropriate to summarize your qualification in the format of a letter rather than submit a resume. Resume letters provide individuals with flexibility in targeting their qualifications to different employers.

- **Make important contacts for developing a critical network of job search relationships.** Networking plays a central role in communicating your goals and marketing your qualifications to others. And letters play a central role in building your network. These letters have two purposes. First, you want to write several letters informing family members, friends, professional acquaintances, and other contacts about your decision to seek new employment. Second, you want them to take action by requesting they refer you to others who might be able to give you additional information, advice, and referrals. You will want to write other letters to strangers in anticipation of developing new relationships relevant to your job search that will also lead to additional information, advice, and referrals. These letters will help you build an important contact list from which you should receive additional advice and referrals. In many cases you should be able to turn these letters into telephone and face-to-face interviews—the prerequisites for getting the critical job interview. We include several examples of these networking or approach letters for your reference. In many respects these are the most im-

portant types of job search letters you will write. They can be amazingly powerful letters that generate quality job leads that lead to job interviews and offers.

- **Express your thoughtfulness and gratitude for receiving assistance from others.** When was the last time you received a thank you letter? How did it make you feel? Chances are you receive few thank you letters, and those you do receive make you feel good. Furthermore, you remember in a positive way those who write a thoughtful thank you letter; these are nice people. In the case of a job search, you must do more than just communicate your qualifications and potential performance to employers. Your values and personal qualities are also important to others who evaluate individuals according to personal criteria. That's what makes you likable— one of the most important qualities determining whether or not you are invited to the job interview and offered the job. Most people prefer associating with individuals they like, who demonstrate gratitude for assistance received, and who acknowledge them as a contributor to their success. You express such values when you write thank you letters in which you express your sincere appreciation for others' assistance and acknowledge them as a contributor to your present and future success. Sending a well-crafted thank you letter may well become the most powerful action you take in your job search.

■ **Get invited to job interviews and receive job offers.** Letters oriented toward persuading others to take action on your behalf are usually follow-up or follow through letters. You send these letters after you have either submitted a resume and/or application or completed a job interview. These letters are expected by the recipient because you mentioned you would follow-up. For example, you should state in the cover letter accompanying your resume a statement of action:

> "I'll call Thursday afternoon, October 20, to see if our schedules would permit a convenient time for us to meet to discuss our mutual interests and my qualifications."

If you call and are unable to reach this individual, you should follow-up with another letter in which you mention your continuing interest in the position and request an interview. This letter should also include another follow-up time. You should follow the same procedure in the case of the job interview. As part of your close to the interview, request permission to follow-up the interview with a telephone call:

> "If I don't hear from you by next Thursday, would it be okay for me to call your office to check on which you plan to make your final decision?"

This request almost always receives an affirmative response. If you call and learn the decision has not been made, send a follow-up letter in which you mentioned you called and reiterate your continuing interest in the position. Also, state that you will call again to inquire about the hiring decision.

## A WORD OF CAUTION

Whatever you do, make sure you write your own job search letters rather than copy or creatively plagiarize examples of others. Indeed, the following pages provide numerous examples of outstanding job search letters designed to communicate information as well as grab the attention of letter recipients. We present them as **examples** for illustrating key writing principles and different types of letters to be written for a variety of job search occasions.

Make sure your letters represent the "unique you" to others. They should express your style and unique qualities. To do otherwise is to engage in deceptive, unethical, or dishonest job search practices. How you write your letters may tell both you and employers how well you are likely to perform on the job. They are partial predictors of your future behavior and on-the-job performance. If you copy others' examples, chances are you also will find unethical or questionable shortcuts to performing your work.

---

*How you write your letters may tell both you and employers how well you are likely to perform on the job.*

---

## CHOOSE THE RIGHT RESOURCES

Each year millions of job hunters turn to career planning books for assistance. Many begin with a general book and next turn to resume and interview books. Others begin with a resume book and later seek other types of job search resources, including letter writing books.

If this book represents your first career planning book, you may want to supplement it with a few other key books. Many of these books are available in your local library and bookstore or they can be ordered directly from Impact Publications by completing the order form at the end of this book. Write for a free copy of the most comprehensive career catalog available today— *"Jobs and Careers for the 1990s. "* To receive the latest edition of this catalog of over 1,000 annotated career resources, simply write

**IMPACT PUBLICATIONS**
ATTN: Free Careers Catalog
9104-N Manassas Drive
Manassas Park, VA 22111-5211

They will send you a copy upon request. Their catalog contains almost every important career and job finding resource available today, including many titles that are difficult if not impossible to find in bookstores and libraries.

Included in this catalog are our other career planning and job search titles that examine critical steps in the job search process as well as careers in special employment fields: *High Impact Resumes and Letters, Dynamite Resumes, Dynamite Cover Letters, Dynamite Answers To Interview Questions, Interview For Success, Network Your Way To Job and Career Success, Discover the Best Jobs For You, Salary Success, The Complete Guide To International Jobs and Careers, The Almanac of International Jobs and Careers, Jobs For People Who Love Travel, Best Jobs For the 1990s and Into the 21st Century, The Almanac of American Government Jobs and Careers, Find a Federal Job Fast, The Complete Guide To Public Employment, Careering and Re-Ca-*

*reering For the 1990s,* and *The Educator's Guide To Alternative Jobs and Careers.*

## NO-NONSENSE WRITING

The following pages are designed to help you create you own powerful job search letters for all types of job search occasions. They are based on the principles outlined in the next chapter as well as those found in our companion volume, *Dynamite Cover Letters.*

If you follow our letter writing principles and develop letters similar to ones outlined in this book, you should be able to create powerful job search letters that command the attention and action of key people involved in your job search, from friends to employers. You will be remembered not only for your qualifications but also for being a thoughtful and likable individual who should be hired. Make sure you incorporate these principles as you create your own set of powerful job search letters!

# Chapter Two

# PITFALLS, PROCESS, AND PRINCIPLES

Writing job search letters follows a well defined process that also incorporates key principles of effective writing. Before you begin creating your own job search letters, let's make sure you have a clear understanding of some major pitfalls as well as the process and its associated principles for effective job search letters. This understanding will help you write your own powerful letters.

## PITFALLS AND PROMISES

Job seekers make many common mistakes when writing letters. These mistakes are the quickest way to kill what should have been an effective job search letter. The most common such mistakes include the following:

- Fails to communicate a clear purpose. In other words, why should the letter recipient read their letter?

- Neglects to link the needs of the letter recipient with the goals of the writer.

- Includes boring contents, reflecting similar approaches used in so many other equally boring letters.

- Looks unprofessional in form, structure, and design.

- Includes spelling, grammatical, and punctuation errors.

- Uses awkward language and the passive voice.

- Overly aggressive, assertive, boastful, hyped, and obnoxious in tone.

- Appears self-centered rather than job or employer-centered.

- Poorly organized, difficult to follow, or wanders aimlessly.

- Says little about the writer's interests, skills, accomplishments, or what they expect to achieve in the future.

- Fails to include adequate contact information.

- Addressed to the wrong person or sent to the wrong place.

- Dull, boring, and uninspired.

- Too long.

- Poorly typed.

- Produced on cheap and unattractive paper.

- Writes only cover letters rather than includes a variety of other equally important job search letters, such as approach and thank you letters, as part of their job search campaign.

- Uses an inappropriate distribution approach such as broadcasting a standard form letter to hundreds of potential employers.

- Closes the letter with the traditional *"I look forward to hearing from you"* closing rather than specify a follow-up action on the part of the letter writer.

- Fails to follow-up letters within one week with a telephone call.

- Handwrites letters rather than type or word process them using a letter quality printer.

- Uses inappropriate stationery and the wrong sized envelope.

- Does not know how to relate job search letters to other equally important job search activities.

Job search letters that avoid these pitfalls may be on the right road to job search success. They at least avoid the trash bin where so many other ineffective job search letters find their final resting place.

## THE PROCESS

Effective job search letters follow certain principles of effective letter writing, production, distribution, and follow-up. Take special note that we include the elements of production, distribution, and follow-up along with writing. For to write a letter without relating it to the next steps in the letter writing process may effectively kill what was otherwise a perfectly good letter.

While the job search should be viewed as a **process** involving specific steps that lead to job interviews and offers, letter writing should also be treated as a process. This process involves four distinct steps:

- **WRITING:** The focus here is only on the rules of letter structure, content, and style—good organization, grammar, spelling, punctuation, and tone. These are elements you learned in English classes as a student—how to write a perfect writing piece. When transferred into the letter medium, the rules of good letter writing also include the use of proper form (full-blocked, square-blocked, modified-blocked, semi-blocked) and structure (heading, date line, inside address, salutation, body, continuation pages, closing, signature line, enclosures, copy reference, postscripts). Given the specific purpose of job search letters—get interviews and job offers—the style and tone of these letters should be closely associated with the style and tone of good advertising copy. Such letters should incorporate these principles of good advertising:

  - Catch the reader's attention.
  - Persuade the reader about you, the product.
  - Convince the reader with more evidence.
  - Move the reader to take action (acquire the product)

- **PRODUCTION:** These principles focus on how you will produce your letters. What type of medium will you use? Will you handwrite, type, or computer-generate your letters? How neat does the final copy look? What type style will you use. If you use a typewriter, will you use a good quality ribbon that produces clear crisp copy? If you use a word processor, will you produce the final copy with a letter quality or laser printer? What type of paper will use you use? What about the color, weight, size, or cotton content of your paper? Will you use personalized stationery or just a plain piece of paper? You need answer these questions and make corresponding decisions **before** you begin sending your letters to specific persons.

- **DISTRIBUTION:** Distribution is a much neglected principle of letter writing. Most letter writers think all they need to do is to properly fold the letter and drop it in the mailbox. However, you should first address some key distribution questions before ending your letter in this manner. For example, what size envelope will you use? How will you label the envelope—handwrite or type the address? Are you planning to use any special delivery services, such as overnight or second-day UPS, Federal Express, or Express Mail services? What type of postage will you affix—stamps or machine affixed postage? How do you plan to distribute cover letters? Broadcast them to hundreds of employers or target them on only a few select employers?

■ **FOLLOW-UP:** Follow-up is the key to getting letter recipients to take action. Without follow-up your letters are likely to result in little or no positive action. You should specify what follow-up actions you will take within a few days after sending your letter. In most cases, follow-up should take the form of a telephone call. It also includes certain types of follow-up letters.

Each of these steps incorporates specific principles that contribute to job search writing success.

# 50 PRINCIPLES THAT MAKE THE PROCESS WORK

Several principles make the job search letter process work. Following each step of the letter process, these principles include the following:

## AUDIENCE

1. Responds to the needs of my audience as indicated from my research on both the organization and the employer.

2. Presents a unique style in both form and content that will be remembered by the letter recipient.

3. Expresses a benefit for the reader that will motivate him to become interested in me and take appropriate action.

## FORM, STRUCTURE, AND DESIGN

4. Makes an immediate good impression on the reader and is inviting to read.

5. Properly incorporates the first seven structural elements of an effective letter—heading, date line, inside address, salutation, body, closing, and signature line.

6. Body of letter is subdivided into two to four paragraphs—but no more.

7. Most paragraphs run no more than five lines.

8. Includes complete name and address of letter recipient.

9. Name is signed firmly and confidently using a pen.

10. Uses a standard typing style.

11. Has a clean, crisp, uncluttered, and professional look.

12. Uses a 1¼ x 1½ inch margin around the top, bottom, and sides.

## ORGANIZATION AND CONTENT

13. Immediately grabs the reader's attention.

14. Presents most important ideas first.

15. Expresses ideas concisely.

16. Relates to the reader's interests and needs.

17. Persuades the reader to take action.

18. Free of spelling, grammatical, and punctuation errors.

19. Incorporates the active voice.

20. Avoids negative words and tones; uses positive language throughout.

21. Expresses the "unique you" rather than approximate the language and content of model letters.

22. Employer-centered rather than self-centered.

23. Stresses benefits the reader is likely to receive from you.

24. Demonstrates a clear purpose.

25. Sentences and paragraphs flow logically and with proper transitions.

26. Includes complete contact information (avoid Post Office box numbers in lieu of a street address).

27. Expresses enthusiasm, energy, and fire.

28. Follows the ABC's of good writing —Always Be Clear, correct, complete, concise, courteous, considerate, creative, cheerful, and careful.

## PRODUCTION

29. Has an overall strong professional appearance sufficient to make an immediate favorable impression.

30. Uses a new or nearly new ribbon (if cloth) with clean keys or printer head.

31. Copy setting adjusted properly so the final copy is not printed too dark or too light.

32. Printed with a standard type style and size.

33. Produced on a letter quality machine.

34. Proofread and ran "spellcheck" (if using a word processing program) for possible spelling/typing errors.

35. Used a good quality paper stock that both looks and feels professional.

36. Selected a paper color appropriate for my audience.

37. Compared to nine other business letters received over the past year, this is one of the best in appearance.

### DISTRIBUTION

38. Addressed to a specific name.

39. Used a No. 10 business or a 9x12" envelope.

40. Checked to make sure all enclosures indeed got enclosed.

41. Matched the envelope paper stock and color to the stationery.

42. Typed address and return address.

43. Affixed a commemorative stamp.

44. Used a special delivery service for overnight delivery in cases where this attention-getting action seemed appropriate.

45. Affixed a U.S. Postal "Priority Mail" sticker on the envelope if mailed in an envelope larger than a No. 10 business envelope.

### FOLLOW-UP

46. Ended letter with an "action statement" indicating I would contact the individual by phone within the next week.

47. Made the first follow-up call at the time and date indicated in my letter.

48. Followed-up with additional phone calls until I was able to speak directly with the person or received the requested information.

49. Maintained a positive and professional attitude during each follow-up activity even after repeated phone calls failed to get through to the letter recipient. Was pleasantly persistent and tactful during all follow-up calls. Never indicated I was irritated, insulted, or disappointed in not having my phone calls returned.

50. Followed-up the follow-up by sending a thank you letter genuinely expressing my appreciation for the person's time and information.

All of these principles are elaborated on, including specific examples, in our other letter writing book, *Dynamite Cover Letters*.

Whatever you do, make sure your letters have the power to persuade others to take action to your benefit. You can do this if you go beyond the writing stage and incorporate the principles of production, distribution, and follow-up in your job search letters.

## LETTERS
## FOR ALL JOB
## SEARCH OCCASIONS

The 201 job search letters appearing in the following pages are designed for all types of job search occasions and situations, from initiating job research to following-up with thank you letters. You can and should write many of these letters at various stages in your job search.

We urge you to examine these letters for ideas on how you can develop the **form and content** of your own job search letters that best represent the "unique you." In each example we've attempted to adhere to our principles of effective letter writing. Please keep in mind there is nothing magical about these examples. Given the example format of this book, we only stress the first stage of letter effectiveness—writing for good form and content. Our examples emphasize how and what to say to individuals in your job search network rather than how, when, where, and with what consequences you will deliver your messages to others. The other stages of letter effectiveness—production, distribution, and follow-up—are the keys to moving your letters into the hands of the right people who will take action that leads to job interviews and offers. It's these other principles you will need to follow as you breathe new life into your job search through the letter writing process.

You will encounter many individuals and find numerous occasions for which you should write a variety of job search letters. The most common ones include:

- **LETTERS TO START YOUR JOB SEARCH:** These letters effectively kick-off your job search into fruitful directions. Your goal at this initial stage should be to gather useful information for developing an effective job search. At this stage you need to contact a variety of groups and individuals: organizations as sources of information on potential employers; organizations as potential employers; publications with job listings; employment services; groups with information on relocation; and organizations with job search resources. These letters may request annual reports, subscription services, contractual services, relocation information, and books and directories. The results of these letters should be a solid database from which to launch an effective job search.

- **LETTERS THAT WILL LAY THE GROUND WORK:** You also need to write several letters for developing important relationships that will hopefully promote your job search. These letters inform others of your job search intentions and activities. They let others know you are in the process of looking for a job, that you welcome advice and referrals, and that you would appreciate that some of your contacts serve as personal and professional references. You address these letters to friends, relatives, acquaintances, professional colleagues, former employers, professors, teachers, ministers, and others who might be willing to serve as a reference or who can provide you with information, advice, or referrals for building your job search network. Many of these letters result in making direct contact with potential employers.

- **LETTERS FOR DEVELOPING CONTACTS AND UNCOVERING JOB LEADS:** The purpose of these letters is to make direct contact with employers for information, advice, referrals, and job interviews. These are the most important "networking" letters you will write. You write many of these letters based on referrals from other individuals. You should also write—"cold turkey" letters—those written directly to employers without a benefit of referrals. Taken together, these letters become the most powerful job search letters you can write for getting a job interview and offer.

- **LETTERS THAT RESPOND TO VACANCY ANNOUNCEMENTS:** These letters address the specific job qualifications and requirements outlined in employers' vacancy announcements. They may or may not accompany a resume and thus become cover letters. While these are the most frequently written job search letters, they are also some of the most ineffective letters. Effective letters direct-

ly respond to position requirements as well as include follow-up actions.

- **COVER LETTERS:** These letters always accompany resumes. They respond to employers' hiring needs as well as clearly highlight the interests and qualifications of the candidate.

- **RESUME LETTERS:** These letters are written in lieu of sending a traditional resume and cover letter. They combine the best elements of both a resume and cover letter.

- **FOLLOW-UP LETTERS:** In many respects these may be the most effective job search letters. They are designed to get employers to take action in reference to your job search activities.

- **THANK YOU LETTERS:** These, too, are some of the most effective job search letters. They communicate an important quality employers readily seek—thoughtfulness. As a result, they set you apart from other job seekers who fail to write such letters. Thank you letters should always be sent to individuals who have provided assistance, be it in the form of information, advice, referrals, or an actual job interview.

- **SPECIAL AND UNUSUAL LETTERS:** A variety of other letters may also be sent during different stages of your job search. Many of these are written for special occasions—offering a solution to an employer's problem, for example. Many are unusual letters that are aimed at getting the attention and action of potential employers. They are unusual for both their medium and message. For example, some of these letters may arrive in the form of a telegram, a formal invitation, a photo-card, an accompanying video, or a card attached to a bouquet of flowers, poster, or a shoebox.

The following chapters are organized according to these various types of job search situations and letters. The examples are based upon the principles outlined earlier in this chapter.

# Chapter Three

# LETTERS TO START YOUR JOB SEARCH

Getting started on your job search can be a difficult task. Where do you start? What should you do? Whom should you contact? These questions can easily be answered by thinking about what needs to be done **first** in order to launch a successful job search.

While some job seekers think they first need a resume or job interview, what they really need is good **information** about the job market, employers, organizations, jobs, job searches, relocation considerations, and resources for managing their job search. While much of this information can be accessed by telephone, well-crafted letters will go a long way in launching a successful job search at this initial stage.

Information gathering letters should be short and to the point. You need not dwell at length about your goals and qualifications. After all, you are seeking information—not a job—at this stage.

Most of these letters can be completed in a few sentences and paragraphs. Keep in mind that your reader is probably a busy person who readily has the information you need. Make his or her job easy by making your request simple and to the point. In some cases you may want to telephone for the information rather than write a letter. Whatever your medium of choice, you still need to gather important job search information **before** sending cover letters and resumes to potential employers.

Letters to start your job search may be aimed at six different information sources. These include letters addressed to:

- organizations as sources of information on potential employers

- organizations as potential employers

- publications with job listings and other job information

- job search, employment, and career assessment services

- groups offering relocation information and services

- organizations with job search resources

Taken together, these "starter" letters identify numerous groups you should consider contacting at the very beginning of your job search. Most will help give direction to your job search. Others emphasize the importance of using group resources in developing an effective job search. And others potentially put you in contact with employers. If you examine the contents of these letters, you should get several useful ideas on how to best organize your job search.

A good way to get your job search launched is to write 25 or more of these letters. The writing exercise itself will help you focus your job search on initial information needs and direct it into fruitful channels. For example, where do you want to live and work during the next five years? If you are considering a move from Boston to Las Vegas, you need to gather information on your targeted community. What's the job outlook like in Las Vegas? Who are the major employers in Las Vegas? What's it like living and working there? Will you have problems finding housing? What's the cost of living in Las Vegas?

If you are staying close to home, you still need to gather information on potential employers. If you are unfamiliar with an organization, write for a copy of their annual report or for other literature on the organization. Contact local employment services to find out what type of services they offer and at what cost and with what performance guarantees. If you need assistance with your job search—from acquiring books to being given a battery of assessment tests—write letters to get this type of information.

The letters presented in this chapter are designed for these six types of initial job search situations. The contents of each outline particular job search needs.

# Requesting Information
(membership listings)

124 Linden Place
Chicago, IL 60002

October 2, 19___

Mindi Mason, Director
ENVIRONMENTAL RESEARCH CENTER
147 Gilbert Avenue
San Francisco, CA 91441

Dear Ms. Mason:

I'm in the process of researching various organizations involved in conducting environmental research on tropical rain forests. Specifically, I'm trying to identify the types of research being conducted as well as the size and location of the various research organizations.

As the national association of environmental research firms, would you have such information available in the form of a membership directory or report?

I would appreciate any assistance you might be able to provide on this subject. Please let me know if there is any charge for this service. Should you wish to contact me by telephone, my number is 312/371-6651.

Sincerely,

Steven Wallace

# Requesting Information
(placement services)

853 West Norton Road
Boise, ID 88344

July 8, 19____

Director
Information Services
ASSOCIATION OF
    AMERICAN ACCOUNTANTS
5391 Tyler Road
Washington, DC 20543

Dear Director:

Does your association provide information on job vacancies with member organizations? As a recent graduate in accounting, I'm interested in contacting firms which are members of your association for employment information.

If you do offer placement services, or publish a newsletter that includes vacancy information, I would appreciate hearing from you. Please send me the necessary information for using your services.

Thank you for your assistance.

Sincerely,

George Miles

## Requesting Information
(alumni network)

973 West End
New York, NY 10001

February 13, 19___

Wanda Evans, Director
Alumni Services
UNIVERSITY OF
   SOUTHERN CALIFORNIA
1933 Jasper Street
Los Angeles, CA 90312

Dear Ms. Evans:

I've been working in New York City with an investment banking firm since graduating from USC in 1987. I'm now in the process of conducting a job search in the Houston area.

I would like to make more contacts with individuals working in and around Houston. Is there a USC alumni group in Houston or does your office have a listing of USC alumni currently residing there?

I would appreciate any assistance you could give me in making contact with fellow alumni. I'm especially interested in acquiring information on job opportunities in the international investment banking field.

Many thanks for your assistance. I look forward to hearing from you.

Sincerely,

Brenda Carpenter

# Requesting Information
### (placement services)

325 Davidson Drive
Baltimore, MD 23153

February 4, 19___

Editor
ASSOCIATION TRENDS
18 St. Elmo Drive
Bethesda, MD 22332

Dear Editor:

I understand you provide a placement and referral service for your
subscribers and readers. In reviewing previous editions of your publication, I
learned this included an "Availability Announcement" section along with a
resume referral service.

If you still provide this service, I would appreciate information on
procedures and costs for being included in the service. Please send me the
information as soon as possible since I want to be included in the next issue.

Thank you for your assistance.

Sincerely,

Janice Forbes

## Requesting Information
(placement services)

246 Cathedral Drive
Salt Lake City, UT 86732

June 3, 19____

James Martin
Association Referral Service
U.S. CHAMBER OF COMMERCE
1615 H St., NW
Washington, DC 20062

Dear Mr. Martin:

I recently learned your office provides placement information and services for your member organizations. I'm especially interested in employment opportunities in Western Europe.

Could you please send me information on your placement services, including any forms I would need to complete and applicable fees?

I appreciate your assistance.

Appreciatively,

Sandra Vertimosa

## Requesting Publications/Data
(targeting job search)

1134 Jackson Place
Sacramento, CA 95243

November 15, 19____

Wilson James, Director
Office of Procurement
Procurement Support Division
AGENCY FOR INTERNATIONAL DEVELOPMENT
1100 Wilson, 14th Floor
Rosslyn, VA 20523

Dear Mr. James:

I understand you now have available the latest editions of the <u>Current Technical Service Contracts and Grants</u> and <u>AID-Financed University Contracts and Grants</u> directories which list all contracts and grants awarded to contractors, nonprofit organizations, and educational institutions by AID during the past three years. I also understand you produce the quarterly <u>Functional Report: Current Indefinite Quantity Contracts</u> report.

I would appreciate it if you could send me the latest editions of these three publications. I know these were previously available at no charge. Should there be a charge, please let me know as soon as possible since it is urgent that I receive them.

Thank you for your kind assistance.

Sincerely,

Martin Grant

## Requesting Company's Annual Report
(via one's stockbroker)

831 Old Town Blvd.
St. Louis, MO 64210

April 7, 19___

John Wilson
SMITH, GRAY, AND WILSON
714 Jefferson Ave., Suite 120
St. Louis, MO 64313

Dear John,

I'm in the process of making a job change and thought you might be able to assist me in gathering information on a firm I'm interested in pursuing— J.C. Williams Company. I know they are listed on the American Stock Exchange.

I would like to know something about the financial outlook of this company. Would it be possible to get me a copy of their annual report as well as any other information on this organization? Who knows, we might decide to buy some stock in the company!

Many thanks for your assistance.

Sincerely,

Mary Stafford

## Requesting Information on Company
(direct contact)

4439 Center Street
Portland, OR 98211

January 30, 19 ___

Melanie Roberts, Director
Public Relations Office
TRC PHARMACEUTICAL COMPANY
1000 West Knight Street
Terre Haute, IN 48732

Dear Ms. Roberts:

I'm in the process of conducting research on various pharmaceutical companies as part of a career development project. Your company was highly recommended as one of the leaders in the field.

Could you please send me information on your company, including an annual report as well as any other information that would help me better understand the future direction of your company? I'm especially interested in learning about your operations in Columbia, Missouri. I enclose a mailing label for your convenience.

Thank you for your assistance.

Sincerely,

Jeffrey Williams

## Requesting Vacancy Announcement
(government agency)

1156 P Street, NW
Washington, DC 20037

December 20, 19___

Fred Teposo
Bureau of Indian Affairs/MS-331 SIB
Branch of Personnel Services/Code 675
1951 Constitution Avenue, NW
Washington, DC 20245

Dear Mr. Teposo:

In reviewing this week's issue of the <u>Federal Job Opportunities Listing</u> I learned you had a vacancy for a Highway Engineer, GS-810-11/12.

Could you please send me a copy of the vacancy announcement (#EAO-90-19) for this position as well as any other information that outlines application procedures? I enclose a mailing label for your convenience.

Thank you for your assistance.

Sincerely,

John Alabroso

# Requesting Information
(subscription)

325 Park Avenue
Indianapolis, IN 47721

August 23, 19___

Manager
Subscription Department
TOLEDO DAILY NEWS
117 S. 47th St.
Toledo, OH 41153

Dear Manager:

I'm planning to move to the Toledo area within the next six months. In preparation for the move, I would like to subscribe to the Sunday edition of the Toledo Daily News which I believe has the most complete weekly listing of employment and real estate classifieds.

Could you please let me know what the subscription procedure and cost would be to receive the Sunday edition? I would like to begin my subscription immediately.

Thank you for your assistance.

Sincerely,

Elizabeth Martino

## Requesting Relocation Information

9341 Capitol Street
Omaha, NE 54371

March 3, 19____

Director
Relocation Department
CENTURY 21
9431 Sheridan Road
Austin, TX 77211

Dear Director:

I will be relocating to the Austin area within the next eight months. Could you send me information on Austin as well as your relocation services?

I'm especially interested in purchasing a home in the $200,000-250,000 range in an area with excellent public schools. I would appreciate any information you could provide me with on both the housing situation and the Austin community.

Sincerely,

Janice Wilson

# Requesting Information
(relocation)

882 Timberlake Rd.
Minneapolis, MN 54371

February 7, 19___

Janice Watson
FIRST CENTURY REAL ESTATE
792 North Adams St.
Suite 319
Knoxville, TN 38921

Dear Ms. Watson:

We plan to move to the Knoxville area within the next six months. Please send us information on your services as well as sample copies of current listings. We would also appreciate any information on Knoxville that would help us better understand the community, such as a directory of churches, schools, and community activities.

We're especially interested in finding a neighborhood with good schools and recreational facilities. We are prepared to look in the price range of $175,000 to $220,000. While we prefer buying, we also would consider renting with an option to buy.

We look forward to working with you in the coming weeks.

Sincerely,

Steven Pollock

## Requesting Relocation Information
(international)

7741 Cedar Lane
Bethesda, MD 20931

May 11, 19____

Janice Lawrence, President
INTERNATIONAL EXPATRIATES
781 Washington Blvd.
Boston, MA 02112

Dear Ms. Lawrence:

I will be moving to Italy within the next six months. In visiting a friend recently, I learned about your wonderful publication—The International Expatriate—for expatriates residing in Europe.

Could you please send me order information on this and any other publications you may have for assisting me with our relocation? We're especially interested in learning more about the schools and employment opportunities in and around Milan.

I appreciate your assistance and look forward to hearing from you.

Sincerely,

Marsha Ventura

## Entering Subscription
(community jobs newspaper)

382 Vancouver Blvd.
Seattle, WA 99311

April 21, 19___

Subscription Manager
THE EMPLOYMENT PAPER
329 2nd Avenue West
Seattle, WA 98119

Dear Subscription Manager:

Could you please enter my subscription for six biweekly issues of The Employment Paper. I enclose a check for $25 to cover the cost of the subscription.

I look forward to receiving my first issue.

Sincerely,

Martin Yost

## Entering Subscription
(federal jobs listing service)

2201 State Street
Albuquerque, NM 83210

August 22, 19____

Circulation Manager
FEDERAL RESEARCH SERVICE
P.O. Box 1059
Vienna, VA 22180

Dear Circulation Manager:

I'm in the process of conducting a job search with the federal government. I understand you publish a biweekly listing of federal job vacancies, offer computer software for completing the SF-171, and conduct job search seminars.

Please send me information on how I can subscribe to Federal Career Opportunities. I'm interested in the six week subscription. I would also appreciate information on any of your other products and services.

Thank you for your assistance.

Sincerely,

Steven Willow

## Requesting Subscription
(international jobs newspaper)

930 West 21st Street
Albany, NY 19999

April 23, 19___

Subscription Manager
INTERNATIONAL EMPLOYMENT GAZETTE
1525 Wade Hampton Blvd.
Greenville, SC 29609

Dear Subscription Manager:

Your publication was highly recommended in the new edition of The Complete Guide to International Jobs and Careers. I'm enclosing a check for $35 to cover the cost of a six-issue subscription. I would appreciate it if you could send me my first issue as soon as possible.

I also understand you operate an international resume writing and referral service. Could you please send me information on this service. I'm particularly interested in finding employment with an accounting firm operating in Europe or the Middle East.

Thank you for your assistance.

Sincerely,

Eileen Young

## Requesting Subscription
(international education/job listings)

9124 Harrison Blvd.
Providence, RI 02412

August 7, 19___

Subscription Manager
THE INTERNATIONAL EDUCATOR
P.O. Box 103
West Bridgewater, MA 02379

Dear Subscription Manager:

Please enter my one-year subscription to The International Educator. I enclose a check for $25 to cover the cost of the four-issue subscription.

Also, please send me the free 16-page booklet—"TIE'S Complete Guide to Finding a Job in an International School"—which comes with my subscription. I'm anxious to get my international job search underway as soon as possible.

Thank you for your assistance.

Sincerely,

Mary Davis

## Developing Connections
(long-distance employers)

771 West Nelson St.
Denver, CO 80121

May 14, 19___

President
CHAMBER OF COMMERCE
444 State Avenue
Phoenix, AZ  89921

Dear President:

   I will be moving to the Phoenix area soon. I would appreciate it if you could send me a directory of your members. I'm especially interested in making contact with retailers who are the major employers in your community.

   Thank you for your assistance.

                                        Sincerely,


                                        Stephanie Adams

## Requesting Resources
(job search directory/catalog)

5187 Terrace Blvd.
Dayton, OH 43281

December 17, 19__

Publisher
IMPACT PUBLICATIONS
9104-N Manassas Drive
Manassas Park, VA 22111

Dear Publisher:

I recently learned about your resource guide, "Jobs and Careers for the 1990s", which includes more than 1000 career resources. I understand this publication is available free of charge.

Could you please send me a copy as soon as possible? I also would like order information on your book, High Impact Resumes and Letters. If you accept credit card orders, please include your fax number so I can place my order by fax.

Sincerely,

Stanley Johnson

# Requesting Order Information
(job search book)

6613 Stevens Point
Detroit, MI 46821

June 1, 19____

Publisher
IMPACT PUBLICATIONS
9104-N Manassas Dr.
Manassas Park, VA 22111

Dear Publisher:

I've been trying to locate a copy of High Impact Resumes and Letters in my local bookstore but with no success. Could you please send me this book as soon as possible since I'm in immediate need of this book for developing my job search?

I enclose a check for $15.95 ($12.95 plus $3.00 shipping) to cover the cost of this book. Please let me know if this is the correct current price. I've been referring to the 1990 edition which I found in our local library.

Sincerely,

Alice Bolton

## Requesting Services
(resume production)

8004 Teasley Court
New Haven, CT 03982

November 21, 19___

Marilyn Jones
FAST RESUMES
421 New York Avenue
New Haven, CT 03980

Dear Ms. Jones:

I understand your company offers resume writing and production services. Could you please send me information on your services so I will have a better idea of how I could best use them?

Since I'm in the process of revising my resume, I would like to know if your company would be able to further strengthen my resume. I enclose a sample copy for your reference.

I specifically need to know the cost for your services and how long it would take before I would have camera-ready copy. Also, do you produce the final copy with matching stationery for cover letters?

I look forward to hearing from you. My phone number is 771-8920.

Sincerely,

Henry Greystone

# Request For Subscription/Referral Services

113 Bellflower Ct.
Orono, ME 08013

August 9, 19____

Subscription Manager
ACCESS: Networking in the
    Public Interest
50 Beacon Street
Boston, MA 02108

Dear Subscription Manager:

I understand you publish a biweekly listing of vacancies with nonprofit organizations as well as offer related job search services to individuals interested in jobs with nonprofit organizations.

I'm interested in reviewing your current vacancy announcements, but I'm not sure where I can gain access to your data base. Which libraries or nonprofit organizations in the Orono area subscribe to your service? I would appreciate it if you could send me information on these organizations. I would also appreciate information on your job matching services which I understand is available on a fee basis to individuals.

Thank you for your assistance.

Sincerely,

Stacey Chino

## Requesting Information/Registering
(temporary employment services)

1134 Stanford Lane
Orlando, FL 31339

July 11, 19____

Janice Eaton
HIGH TEMPS
73 Weston Road
Suite 913
Orlando, FL 31341

Dear Ms. Eaton:

I am interested in a temporary position in word processing. As my enclosed resume indicates, I have over seven years of progressively responsible experience working with a variety of software programs. During the past three years I have extensively used the newest versions of WordPerfect.

Could you please send me information on how I might work with your organization? I assume you have signed contracts with those who register with your firm. Please send me information about your organization as well as the necessary forms for registration.

I would appreciate it if you could keep my resume on file for future reference. Should a position become available for someone with my experience, I would appreciate hearing from you.

I will give you a call next week to answer any questions you might have concerning my interests and background.

Sincerely,

Martin Davis

# Requesting Job Search Services

5431 Atlanta Blvd.
Atlanta, GA 33479

May 9, 19____

Thomas Allen
HALDANE ASSOCIATES
848 Peachtree Plaza
Atlanta, GA 33481

Dear Mr. Allen:

I am in the process of making a career change. During the past seven years I have worked in the field of education as a Speech Therapist. I'm interested in leaving education to pursue a career in the private sector.

A friend recommended that I contact you concerning your career transition services. She mentioned you were one of the leading firms providing such career assistance.

I would appreciate it if you would provide me with information on your services. I especially need to know how you operate with clients including career counseling, testing, and placement services. I would like to know what types of contractual arrangements I would I be entering for what period of time, the costs of your services, and how many job interviews and offers I might expect during the contract period.

I would also appreciate it if you could provide me with the names and telephone numbers of three former clients who have successfully used your services.

I enclose a copy of my resume for your reference. I have a strong teaching and research background which I need to relate to jobs and careers outside education. Please let me know if the services of your company would be appropriate for someone with my background.

Sincerely,

Paul Martinez

## Contacting Executive Search Firm

1367 River Run Dr.
Burke, VA 23222

September 17, 19____

Maryann Philips
EXECUTIVE SEARCH UNLIMITED
821 Shore Drive
Suite 913
Miami, FL 32193

Dear Ms. Philips:

I understand you specialize in recruiting chemical engineers in the international environmental field. During the past five years I have worked with the Environmental Protection Agency as a policy analyst in its Office of International Affairs. I've had a unique opportunity to apply chemical engineering skills to important international policy issues.

I plan to leave government for the private sector within the next 18 months. I'm interested in the possibility of working with an international contracting and consulting firm in the environmental field. Since this is an area in which you recruit, I would appreciate it if you could keep my resume on file for future reference.

Please let me know if you need any additional information on my background and availability.

Sincerely,

Debra Follett

## Contacting Resume Bank Service

752 Thompson Court
Albany, NY 14321

March 23, 19_____

James Reston
HEALTH SYSTEMS RECRUITERS, INC.
918 Monroe Street
Chicago, IL 60021

Dear Mr. Reston:

Mary Allen suggested that I send you a copy of my resume. She said you specialized in recruiting health care administrators for HMOs.

I have nine years of progressive experience in administering two medium-sized health care facilities in upper state New York. Within the next two years I hope to relocate to the southwest, preferably a major metropolitan area in Arizona or southern California.

I enclose a copy of my resume for your reference. Mary Allen mentioned you maintain a resume bank of potential candidates for your clients. I would appreciate it if you could keep me on file for future reference.

Please let me know if you need any additional information.

Sincerely,

Doris Luffert

## Screening Employment Services

8801 West End St.
Cleveland, OH 45313

December 29, 19___

President
JOBS ABROAD
203 Ocean Blvd.
Ft. Lauderdale, FL 31111

Dear President:

I noticed your ad in the Cleveland Plain Dealer for information on job opportunities in Australia. I'm curious as to what you have to offer since I understand the current unemployment rate in Australia is nearly 15 percent.

I would appreciate it if you could send me information on your product or service. If you are one of the firms selling a video accompanied by a listing of Australian employers, or if you require up-front fees for promised job placements, please do not reply to this letter. I'm only interested in contacting a bona fide firm that is retained by employers.

Sincerely,

Daryl Peterson

## Contacting Potential Employer
(resume bank)

452 North Belmont
Franklin, KY 42012

October 23, 19____

Gerald Davidson
AGRICULTURAL EDUCATION
  SERVICES INTERNATIONAL
2314 23rd Street, NW
Washington, DC 20123

Dear Mr. Davidson:

I'll complete my Ph.D. in agricultural economics from the University of Kentucky within the next six months. While conducting my dissertation research in the Philippines last year, I met two of your staff members who were working from your Davao City regional office—Steven Chambers and Allan Able. They suggested I send you a copy of my resume for your reference.

I understand you maintain a resume bank you refer to for candidates to staff upcoming projects. I would like to be included in it as well as considered for future projects relating to the Philippines or other countries in which you work.

I'm especially interested in developing marketing systems relating to irrigation cooperatives. My dissertation research has focused on the role of revolving funds in irrigation cooperatives as they relate to developing new agricultural marketing mechanisms for developing countries. This is an area the World Bank and the Agency For International Development have indicated a strong interest in developing pilot projects in fifteen countries during the next five years.

I would appreciate an opportunity to discuss with you and your staff how my work might be developed into new project proposals for these organizations. I'll call your office next Thursday to see if you have any questions concerning my background and interests.

Sincerely,

Sandra Alliston

## Requesting Information
(testing and assessment services)

891 Davis Blvd.
Austin, TX 71311

September 4, 19___

Janet Evans, President
CAREER TESTING SERVICES, INC.
234 Warner Drive
Austin, TX 71312

Dear Ms. Evans:

I'm in the process of re-entering the job market after nearly ten years as a homemaker. When I attended high school nearly 20 years ago, I took a battery of tests to determine my occupational interests, skills, and abilities. I'm sure my interests, skills, and abilities have changed considerably since that time.

I understand you administer similar tests that are more current and perhaps more useful for today's job market. Could you send me information on what types of testing services you offer, including your fee schedule?

Thank you for your assistance.

Sincerely,

Martha Vestal

## Requesting Information
(job search services)

8901 Taylor Road
Birmingham, AL 32112

April 2, 19____

Alice Steves, Director
THE WOMEN'S CENTER
7742 Federal Avenue
Birmingham, AL 32114

Dear Ms. Steves:

I learned from a recent article in the <u>Daily News</u> that you offer job and career assistance. Since I've been out of the job market for several years, I'm really interested in learning about job alternatives for someone with my background. I also need to get a better idea of what I'm best qualified to do as well as write a resume.

Could you please send me information on the services available through your center? For example, do you offer individualized testing and assessment services and courses on how to write resumes and interview for jobs? I would be interested in knowing how I can best use the Women's Center for conducting a job search.

I appreciate your assistance and look forward to working with you and your staff.

Sincerely,

Janice Furniss

## Requesting Information
(job search assistance)

882 West 23rd Street
Kansas City, MO 64444

May 11, 19___

Jill Mason, Director
40-PLUS OF KANSAS CITY
1133 Truman Blvd.
Kansas City, MO 64444

Dear Ms. Mason:

I will shortly become unemployed because my company, where I've worked for nearly 20 years, decided to relocate to Florida. I'm now in the process of looking for an executive level position with a company in the Kansas City area.

One of my close friends highly recommended that I contact you. She found her current job while participating in your group several years ago.

I understand you provide a variety of job search services for individuals in my situation. Could you please send me information on your organization and how I might participate? Since my last day of work will be next Friday, I'm prepared to conduct a job search on a full-time basis. Any assistance Forty-Plus of Kansas City could give me would be greatly appreciated.

Sincerely,

David Fortina

## Requesting Job Search Assistance

1134 West Ford Ave.
Dallas, TX 73112

August 14, 19____

Dr. Delores Clements
DALLAS COMMUNITY COLLEGE
Career Counseling Center
241 Lone Star Blvd.
Dallas, TX 73110

Dear Dr. Clements:

A friend informed me that your Center offers a variety of job search courses and services that are open to the general public.

I've been unemployed during the past three months. So far my efforts at landing a job have not been successful. At this point I think I need some professional guidance to help get my job search on track.

Could you send me information on what types of courses and services you offer? I probably need some testing and assessment work. And I know I could use some assistance on improving my resume.

Sincerely,

Martin Morrison

## Requesting Information
(career training and placement services)

722 Georgetown Road
Washington, DC 20134

February 18, 19____

Director
SATOTRAVEL ACADEMY
1005 N. Glebe Road
First Floor
Arlington, VA 22201

Dear Director:

I saw your ad in yesterday's edition of <u>The Washington Post</u>. I'm interested in pursuing a career in the travel industry, preferably with one of the major airlines.

Could you please send me information on your training programs? I'm especially interested in learning more about the duration and costs of training as well as your placement services.

I look forward to receiving information on your programs.

Sincerely,

Nina Barton

# Chapter Four

# LAYING ESSENTIAL GROUND WORK

---

While the letters in Chapter Three were primarily designed to gather information for directing your job search into fruitful channels, the letters in this chapter will help you develop important relationships for promoting your job search. Most of these letters are addressed to people you already know but who may not know you are in the process of looking for a job. More than just a collection of job search letters, these letters represent important job search activities you should engage in at the very beginning of your job search.

One of your first job search activities should be to contact individuals who may be helpful to you in looking for employment. These individuals may include friends, relatives, acquaintanc-es, professional colleagues, former employers, professors, teachers, ministers, or any other people who might serve as either a professional or personal reference or who may be able to provide you with information, advice, or referrals relevant to your job search. These also include your college placement office.

## REFERENCES

At the very start of your job search you need to begin thinking about persons you want to ask to serve as your references. After all, some time during your job search, usually during the job interview, you will be asked for references. While many employers never check these references, others will.

Make sure the individuals you designate as your references know about your job search. They should be informed that you are looking for a job. They should have a copy of your resume on file along with a letter that outlines your plans and asks permission to use them as a reference. You should also keep them informed of your job search progress. If you know you are likely to be interviewed for a job, let them know about the specific job so they have some idea of the type of position you will be seeking. The more information you can provide them on your goals and the specific position, the better prepared they should be to give you a strong recommendation.

## ANNOUNCING YOUR INTENTIONS

The process of developing contacts and job leads or networking involves contacting numerous people. One of the most important groups for developing your networks consists of individuals you already know. These may consist of the following:

- Friends (take a look at your Christmas card list)
- Neighbors (current and past)
- Social acquaintances: social club members, tennis, golf, swim, PTA members
- Classmates—from any level of school
- College alumni (Get a list of those living near you)

- Teachers—your college professors, your childrens' teachers
- Anybody you wrote a check to in the past year:
  - tradespeople, drugstore owner
  - doctor, dentist, optician
  - lawyer, accountant, real estate agent
  - insurance agent, stock broker, travel agent
- Manager of local branch of your bank
- Present and former co-workers
- Relatives
- Politicians (local leaders often are businessmen/women or professionals in town who seem to know everybody.)
- Chamber of Commerce executives in town
- Pastors, ministers (excellent resources)
- Members of your church
- People you meet at conventions
- Speakers at meetings you've attended
- Business club executives and members (Rotary, Kiwanis, Jaycees, Inc.)
- Representatives of direct-sales business (real estate, insurance, Amway Shaklee, Avon)

After developing your comprehensive list of contacts, classify the names into different categories of individuals:

- Those in influential positions or who have hiring authority

- Those with job leads

- Those most likely to refer you to others

- Those with long-distance contacts

Select at least 25 names from your list for initiating your first round of contacts. Your letters to these individuals informing them of your job search intentions and requesting assistance in the form of advice and referrals will initiate your prospecting and networking campaign which should eventually lead to informational interviews, formal job interviews, and job offers. These letters may well become your most important job search letters. They give direction to the core dynamics for finding jobs on the hidden job market—prospecting and networking.

## EXPRESSING YOUR SINCERE GRATITUDE

Be sure to write thank you letters any time someone assists you with your job search. These letters should be routinely sent in cases when someone gives you advice or referrals or who indicates their willingness to serve as a professional or personal reference. These letters communicate **thoughtfulness** to others—one of the most important qualities you should continuously express throughout your job search. Thank you letters can make the different between getting active advice and referrals or getting only perfunctory

*"best wishes with your job search"* responses. Indeed, many job seekers and employers report thank you letters to be more important to getting a job than other types of job search letters.

## Requesting Information
(organizing placement files)

248 Buchanan St., Apt. 201
Flint, MI 48321

September 21, 19___

Susan Strousburg, Director
Career Planning and Placement
UNIVERSITY OF DETROIT
Detroit, MI 47315

Dear Ms. Strousburg:

I'm a 1990 graduate of the University of Detroit with a B.S. in biology. During the past two years I've worked in several part-time positions. I'm now in the possess of seeking a full-time position, preferably with the pharmaceutical industry.

I anticipate contacting numerous employers and interviewing for several positions during the next three months. However, I believe I need to update my placement file since several changes have taken place during the past three years.

Could you send me the necessary forms for updating my file? I probably need to include new references. Also, does your office provide job search assistance for alumni? If so, what type of assistance might I receive? I'll call your office next week to check on my file and these questions.

I appreciate your assistance.

Sincerely,

Jeffrey Taylor

## Requesting Reference
(former teacher)

9113 Stanford Road
Milton, PA 18722

January 4, 19____

Professor Martin Stone
Department of English
UNIVERSITY OF PITTSBURGH
Pittsburgh, PA 17231

Dear Professor Stone:

It has been nearly three years since we last discussed the role of creative writing in business communication. I remember so well your advice on developing other-directed goals in all forms of communication. It has helped me on numerous occasions to better organize thoughts and messages in my daily work—even though I've spoken more Spanish than English during the past two years!

Since completing my BA three years ago, I joined the Peace Corps and served as a Volunteer in Guatemala. I taught English as a foreign language in a small high school near Guatemala City and even helped develop an English club which became popular in our community. Three of my students did so well that they are now foreign exchange students in the States.

While I very much enjoyed my Volunteer experience, I must now turn my attention to more long-term career concerns. As you can see from my enclosed resume, I'm hoping to find a high school English teaching position—preferably in the Philadelphia area.

I would appreciate it if you could serve as one of my references. I enclose a reference form requested from the university placement office. Could you please complete this form and return it to the placement office as soon as possible? I enclose a self-addressed stamped envelope for your convenience.

I really appreciate your assistance with this matter. I'm hoping to have my placement file complete within the next two weeks and shortly thereafter begin interviewing for positions. Should you hear of any vacancies for someone with my qualifications, please feel free to pass my name and resume on to interested parties.

I hope to be in the Pittsburgh area sometime next month. Perhaps we could get together briefly over a cup of coffee. I'm anxious to learn what's been happening in the department during the past three years.

Sincerely,

Janet Stillman

## Requesting Reference/Contacts
(former employer)

643 Nellum Street
Knoxville, TN 34822

April 9, 19___

Susan Jacobson, President
JACOBSON AND TYLER ADVERTISING
239 Wabash Street
Chicago, IL 60003

Dear Susan,

Since leaving Chicago three years ago, I've been working for a small advertising company here in Knoxville—J. C. Thompson. I've very much enjoyed the work. Indeed, I've done some of my most creative work during these past 18 months.

I will be re-entering the job market within the next six months. My present employers have decided to retire after nearly 30 years of business. Since the local economy has negatively impacted advertising, it does not appear the firm will be sold to an outside investor. Consequently, we are all preparing to say "Goodbye". At the same time, I've decided to move to Seattle to be closer to my parents who are now in their mid-80s. I'll be seeking a position in advertising in the Seattle Metro area.

I immediately thought of you as I began planning for this move. I remember how helpful you were in connecting me with my current position for which I am very grateful. Could I again call on you for advice and assistance?

- Do you know anyone in the Seattle-Vancouver area who might be interested in my background?

- Could I use your name as a reference?

I enclose a copy of my resume for your information. Please feel free to pass it on to anyone who might be interested in my qualifications.

Will you be attending the National Conference on Media Advertising in San Francisco next month? Marilyn and I will be there for four days, (May 15-18). We'll be staying at the Omni International. It would be great to see you again and perhaps get together for lunch or dinner. Marilyn says she knows some wonderful seafood restaurants you'll just love!

Sincerely,

Bill McDonald

## Requesting Reference
(minister)

7231 Delaware Street
Winston-Salem, NC 39482

March 19, 19___

Rev. George C. Allen
CHURCH OF CHRIST
984 Angelical Avenue
Winston-Salem, NC 39482

Dear Rev. Allen:

As you may know, I will be graduating from Central High School in June. In September I will attend the University of North Carolina in Chapel Hill where I plan to major in dental hygiene. Between June and September I'm hoping to land a summer job that will enable me to save money for next year's college expenses.

Would you be so kind as to serve as a personal reference? Since I have very little work experience, potential employers will probably want to know something about my personal character. I thought of you as a reference because I've been very active in our church youth group. I believe you more than anyone else has had a chance to observe me working with others.

I appreciate your assistance. Should an employer ask for a reference, I will give them your name and telephone number.

Sincerely,

Margaret Davis

### Informing About Job Search/
### Requesting Advice and Referrals

711 W. End St.
New York, NY 10023

January 4, 19___

Darlene Mason
213 Camelback Road
Phoenix, AZ 89241

Dear Darlene,

I just received our alumni bulletin and noticed you now live in Phoenix. What a coincidence. My husband John and I will be moving to Phoenix in April. His company, Sontana Electronics, transferred him to their Phoenix research center.

It will be good to see you again and catch up on the last ten years of our lives. I always remember our late night dorm sessions when be talked at length about what we were going to do when we graduated. Now we should have some really good stories!

I'm sure you could give us some great "Phoenix" tips. One of my major concerns will be looking for a job. During the past five years I have been working part-time as a management trainer. Now that our children are in school, I plan to look for a full-time training position. Should you know of firms that hire for such positions, I would appreciate learning about them. I'm trying to make as many contacts as possible with potential employers before we make the move in April.

We're really looking forward to our move to Phoenix—and seeing you again.

Sincerely,

Margaret Benton

## Informing About Job Search/
## Requesting Advice and Referrals

203 Jason Drive
Columbia, MO 67332

July 2, 19___

Janice Peterson
Guidance Department
JEFFERSON COUNTY HIGH SCHOOL
492 West County Road
Columbia, MO 68221

Dear Ms. Peterson:

It's been nearly four years since I last saw you. I remember how helpful you were when I was trying to decide on my career direction.

As you know, I joined the U.S. Navy immediately after graduation. I've had a chance to learn a great deal during this time, from becoming a communications specialist to having a chance to travel to many parts of Europe and the Middle East. It's been a very interesting and rewarding four years.

I'll be leaving the Navy in another six months. My plans are to return to Columbia and get a job. I'm also hoping to attend junior college on a part-time basis. I eventually want to get my degree in computer science.

I'm really not sure where to start my job search in Columbia. Do you have any suggestions? I enclose a draft of my resume for your reference. Perhaps you know some employers who might be interested in my qualifications. I would appreciate any leads you are able to share with me.

I look forward to seeing you again when I return to Columbia.

Sincerely,

Margaret Snyder

## Requesting Advice and Referrals

**GERALD S. SNYDER**

782 South Street ▪ Seattle, WA 98322 ▪ 802/731-9228

August 3, 19____

John Turner
STATE FARM INSURANCE
993 Colony Terrace
Seattle, WA 98321

Dear John,

I wanted to let you know that I'm in the process of changing jobs. I'm leaving R.J. Systems after four years of increasingly responsible sales and marketing experience. Jane and I plan to remain in Seattle.

Do you know of any employers in the Seattle area that would be interested in my sales and marketing background? Perhaps you might have some suggestions as to whom I might contact. I enclose a copy of my resume for your reference.

I'll give you a call next week.

Sincerely,

Jerry Walsh

## Expressing Gratitude For Reference

481 Alliance Street
Milford, MA 02189

February 21, 19___

Professor Stanley Friar
Department of Engineering
UNIVERSITY OF MASSACHUSETTS
Amherst, MA 03192

Dear Professor Friar:

Thank you so much for helping me complete my placement file. The placement center informed me that my file is now complete. I know you are very busy and completing recommendation forms is quite time consuming.

I'm sure your recommendation will assist me greatly with my job search. In fact, my first job interview is scheduled for next week. I'll be interviewing for an entry-level position with R. C. Jameson, Inc., a Boston-based engineering firm specializing in urban mass transit design. They are doing the type of work I'm most interested in pursuing at this initial stage of my career.

I'll keep you informed on my progress.

Sincerely,

April Carter

## Expressing Gratitude For Job Search Advice

9912 Cortney Place
Bethesda, MD 20999

March 2, 19____

Sarah Allison
839 P Street, NW
Washington, DC 20032

Dear Sarah,

Thanks so much for your advice on contacting professional associations for editing opportunities in the publishing industry. Concentrating primarily on local newspapers and magazines, I hadn't thought of these groups as "publishers."

What a pleasant surprise it was to discover that several associations headquartered in Alexandria, Virginia operate huge publishing programs. They produce monthly newsletters and magazines with circulations in excess of 500,000 as well as operate large book publishing divisions. Best of all, many are regularly seeking editing talent.

I've contacted several associations in the Washington, DC area during the past few days. The ones that most interest me are doing exciting work in the health care and environmental areas. I'm developing some good contacts with these organizations that I hope will turn into job interviews.

Without your advice I would have over-looked what appear to be some of country's major publishers. Thanks for helping me re-direct by job search focus. I'll keep you posted as to where all this leads.

Sincerely,

James Patterson

## Expressing Gratitude For Job Referral

8123 Park Avenue
Albuquerque, NM 84913

May 17, 19___

Vivien Parker
452 Albert Street
Albuquerque, NM 84909

Dear Vivien,

You were right! Margaret Easton knows her stuff. What a wonderful person to meet and learn from.

She was really helpful in giving me advice on whom to contact for possible job openings in the paralegal field. She also shared some of her "inside" observations on which firms I should avoid. I did not know, for example, that several major law firms are currently reducing their staffs.

She suggested that I focus my job search on a few small law firms specializing in environmental law. It's a growing legal area I'm very interested in. She made some good suggestions on how I could strengthen my resume for such firms. She also referred me to three firms which I've contacted; two will interview me next week.

I enclose a copy of my revised resume for your reference. I think it better represents my goals than the one I gave you a few weeks ago.

Thanks again for recommending that I contact Ms. Easton for information and advice. She may be responsible for my landing my next job!

Sincerely,


Janice Davidson

# *Chapter Five*

# DEVELOPING CONTACTS AND JOB LEADS

How do you plan to approach employers? What approach will you use to communicate your qualifications to them? Will you primarily respond to want ads and vacancy announcements with cover letters and resumes or will you make cold telephone calls or directly contact employers with unsolicited resumes and letters?

In this chapter we examine several letters used for approaching employers. Whereas application and cover letters primarily respond to want ads or vacancy announcements, approach letters are usually not written with a particular job vacancy in mind. Their purpose is to **develop contacts** which may or may not lead to useful information, advice, and referrals. Eventually many of these letters pay off by making contacts with employers who have jobs appropriate for your interests, skills, and abilities.

## POWERFUL LETTERS

Approach letters are some of the most powerful job search letters you will ever write. While most job seekers are preoccupied with writing cover letters to accompany resumes, few job seekers ever write approach letters. These letters are so important that we recommend you spend at least 35 percent of your writing time producing approach letters. They become your calling card for opening the doors to potential employers.

## NETWORKING
## NUTS AND BOLTS

Approach letters build and extend job search networks that are the key to uncovering jobs that best fit your interests, skills, and motivations. They are the job search equivalent to the prospecting and networking activities engaged in by salespeople to expand and build their client base. You will expand and build your networks by writing and following-up the many approach letters you should write throughout your job search.

Approach letters communicate your interests, skills, and motivations to others—who may or may not be potential employers—in a low-keyed manner. In contrast to cover letters and resumes that basically ask for a job, approach letters primarily seek information, advice, and referrals. These are non-threatening letters since they do not put individuals on the spot by asking them for a job.

## TWO BASIC FORMS

Approach letters come in two basic forms—cold turkey and referral. **Cold turkey approach letters** are the written equivalent to a cold telephone call. These letters are written to individuals without the benefit of a prior contact. The best such letters attempt to find some common ground from which to link the writer's interests and goals to those of the letter recipient.

**Referral approach letters** are written with the benefit of a contact person. You link yourself to the letter recipient by way of someone he or she knows and hopefully respects. Depending on the quality of the referral, this contact person may result in instant access to the letter recipient who feels obligated to grant you an informational interview or at least give you information, advice, and referrals over the telephone. In other cases the referral is for the purpose of identifying a possible job opening.

The major purpose of both types of approach letters is the same—get information, advice, and referrals from the letter recipient. Information, advice, and referrals are the key elements for building job search networks that lead to employers who have the type of job you are looking for. If you fail to write these letters, you will neglect one of the most fruitful avenues for uncovering job leads and landing the right job for you.

We also include examples of approach letters that are aimed at possible job openings. Written as either cold turkey or referral approach letters, these letters go beyond the less subtle information and advice gathering letters. They frankly ask the letter recipient if he or she has or knows of a job opening for someone with your interests, skills, and experience. The cold turkey version of these types of approach letters are similar to cold telephone calls used by salespeople engaged in prospecting for new clients.

## ROLE OF RESUMES

Examine the following letters carefully. Keep in mind the clear purpose of each letter—acquire useful information, advice, and referrals rather than arrange a job interview or ask for a job. Unfortunately, many writers of approach letters get confused about their purpose and thus make the mistake of putting the letter recipient on the spot by asking for a job. Furthermore, many writers enclose their resume with these letters—a clear sign they are confused about what they are doing. Regardless of what you say in your letter, an enclosed resume indicates you are looking for a job. The resume, in effect, turns the approach letter into a cover letter. It weakens the impact of the approach letter and thus effectively kills it as a networking device.

Resumes should never accompany an approach letter. In this situation the resume is best shared with the letter recipient at the end of a face-to-face informational interview. This interview should be the ultimate goal of your approach letter—schedule a meeting wherein you interview the individual to gain information, advice, and referrals. It is only at the very end of this interview that you should share your resume with the individual—ask him or her to critique it. In addition to gaining important information, advice, and job lead referrals, your approach letters should eventually result in an improved resume. It will reflect the thoughtful advice received from those who granted you an informational interview.

For more information on the role of letters and resumes in networking activities as well as the informational interview, see two of our other career books—*Network Your Way to Job and Career Success* and *Interview For Success*.

## TAKING ACTION

Similar to other job search letters, approach letters require you to take initiative in contacting the letter recipient for a meeting. Make sure you end your letter with a statement concerning what action you will take next and when the person can expect to hear from you. In most cases referral approach letters will result in scheduling a face-to-face meeting. Expect nearly 50 percent of cold turkey approach letters to result in either a face-to-face meeting or a telephone conversation with the letter recipient. If you mistakenly enclose your resume with an approach letter, expect your response rate to decline dramatically. Despite what you say in your letter about only seeking information and advice, a resume accompanying an approach letter says *"I'm looking for a job—do you have one?"* Few people are interested in spending valuable time talking to applicants who ostensibly approach them for information and advice but who only want to "use" them for getting a job.

# Referral
(information and advice)

1099 Seventh Avenue
Akron, OH 44522

December 10, 19___

Janet L. Cooper, Director
Architectural Design Office
RT ENGINEERING ASSOCIATES
621 West Grand Avenue
Akron, OH 44520

Dear Ms. Cooper:

John Sayres suggested that I write to you regarding my interest in architectural drafting. He thought you would be a good person to give me some career advice.

I am interested in an architectural drafting position with a firm specializing in commercial construction. As a trained draftsman, I have six years of progressive experience in all facets of construction, from pouring concrete to developing plans for $14 million in commercial and residential construction. I am particularly interested in improving construction design and building operations of shopping complexes.

Mr. Sayres mentioned you as one of the leading experts in this growing field. Would it be possible for us to meet briefly? Over the next few months I will be conducting a job search. I am certain your counsel would assist me as I begin looking for new opportunities.

I will call your office next week to see if your schedule permits such a meeting.

Sincerely,

John Albert

## Cold Turkey
(information and advice)

2189 West Church Street
New York, NY 10011

May 3, 19_____

Patricia Dotson, Director
NORTHEAST ASSOCIATION
  FOR THE ELDERLY
9930 Jefferson Street
New York, NY 10013

Dear Ms. Dotson:

I have been impressed with your work with the elderly. Your organization takes a community perspective in trying to integrate the concerns of the elderly with those of other community groups. Perhaps other organizations will soon follow your lead.

I am anxious to meet you and learn more about your work. My background with the city Volunteer Services Program involved frequent contact with elderly volunteers. From this experience I decided I preferred working primarily with the elderly.

However, before I pursue my interest further, I need to talk to people with experience in gerontology. In particular, I would like to know more about careers with the elderly as well as how my background might best be used in the field of gerontology.

I am hoping you can assist me in this matter. I would like to meet with you briefly to discuss several of my concerns. I will call next week to see if your schedule permits such a meeting.

I look forward to meeting you.

Sincerely,

Carol Timms

## Referral
(information and advice)

235 W. Charles St.
Baltimore, MD 21200

July 26, 19___

Craig Allen
T. ROWE PRICE ASSOCIATES, INC.
100 East Pratt Street
Baltimore, MD 21202

Dear Mr. Allen:

Jerry Weitz recommended that I contact you about my interests in Graphic Design. He spoke highly of you and said you might be able to give me some useful advice on job opportunities for someone with my background and interests.

Two years ago I completed my Bachelor's degree in Graphic Design. Since then I've been working as a graphic designer at L. C. Printing Company where I've acquired invaluable experience in all phases of graphic design and production. I have a working knowledge of offset printing and have worked extensively with the MacIntoch Computer and QuarkXPress software.

Mr. Weitz said you have been working with one of the country's leading investment firms during the past seven years as a publications oriented graphic designer. I'm interested in learning more about career opportunities with corporations seeking to develop in-house graphic design capabilities. Would it be possible to meet briefly to discuss my career interests? Since my experience has been limited to the printing industry, I'm sure I could learn a great deal from you.

I'll call you on Wednesday afternoon to see if your schedule would permit such a meeting. I really appreciate whatever information and advice you could give me.

Sincerely,

Laura Baker

## Cold Turkey
(information and advice)

136 West Davis St.
Washington, DC 20030

October 2, 19___

Sharon T. Avery
Vice President for Sales
BENTLEY ENTERPRISES
529 W. Sheridan Road
Washington, DC 20011

Dear Ms. Avery:

I am writing to you because you know the importance of having a knowledgeable, highly motivated, and enthusiastic sales force market your fine information processing equipment. I know because I have been impressed with your sales representatives.

I am seeking your advice on how I might prepare for a career in your field. I have a sales and secretarial background—experience acquired while earning may way through college.

Within the coming months I hope to begin a new career. My familiarity with word processing equipment, my sales experience, and my Bachelor's degree in communication have prepared me for the information processing field. I want to begin in sales and eventually move into a management level position.

As I begin my job search, I am trying to gather as much information and advice as possible before applying for positions. Could I take a few minutes of your time next week to discuss my career plans? Perhaps you could suggest how I can improve my resume—which I am now drafting—and who might be interested in my qualifications. I will call you on Monday to see if such a meeting can be arranged.

I appreciate your consideration and look forward to meeting you.

Sincerely,

Gail S. Topper

## Referral
(information and advice)

### SAMUAL ROLLINS

782 N. Davis              Raleigh, NC 27832              831/782-4813

June 28, 19____

Janet O'Brien
JAMES, ALLEN, AND O'BRIEN
8132 Broadway
Washington, DC 20031

Dear Ms. O'Brien:

Mary Varner recommended that I contact you concerning my plans to relocate
to the Washington, D.C. area. She said you would be a good person to talk
with concerning my interests in contacting firms specializing in environmental
law.

While completing my law degree at Emory University, I became very interested
in environmental law. Many of the cases I reviewed involved law firms,
lobbyists, nonprofit environmental groups, and federal agencies located in
Washington, D.C. Not surprising, I concluded the nation's capital is obviously
the center for anyone interested in pursuing a career in environmental law.

I'll be visiting Washington the week of July 23. Would it be possible to get
together briefly to discuss my career interests. I know I could learn a great deal
from your experience and would appreciate any information, advice, and
referrals you might give me on opportunities in environmental law. I'll call you
next Thursday to see if your schedule would permit such a meeting.

I look forward to meeting you.

                                              Sincerely,

                                              Samuel Rollins

## Cold Turkey
(information and advice)

**MARTIN L. POTTER**

632 Old Gates Road          Landover, MD 23219          410/392-9231

March 17, 19___

Thomas Nelson
ACT TRAINING SYSTEMS
719 Wilson Blvd.
Arlington, VA 21313

Dear Mr. Nelson:

As a fellow member of the American Society For Training and Development, I've admired your work in expanding the involvement of technical trainers in our local ASTD chapter. Indeed, our April symposium on "Developing Needs Assessment in Technical Training" was one of the most useful meetings I've ever attended. It gave me several new ideas I've been able to incorporate in my own professional development.

During the past five years I've been working as a technical trainer with the Department of Navy. I specialize in computer programming of communication systems. While I've very much enjoyed my work with the Navy, it's now time I begin looking at career options in the private sector. I'm especially interested in working with a small consulting firm—preferably one which does contact work with the government—specializing in technical training.

Would your schedule during the next few weeks permit a few minutes to meet with me to discuss my career interests? Having been out of the job market for several years, I would value your advice on how I might best approach the private sector with my technical training interests and skills.

I'll call your office on Thursday afternoon to see if such a meeting would be possible.

Sincerely,

Geraldine West

## Cold Turkey
(information and advice)

9231 Taylor Avenue
Cincinnati, OH 43821

February 3, 19___

Marsha Sullivan, Director
COMMUNITY ACTION FOR SENIORS
812 Fairview Blvd., Suite 201
Cincinnati, OH 43820

Dear Ms. Sullivan:

Congratulations on receiving the annual Jaycee's Community Service Award for your work in developing recreational facilities for the elderly. I've been especially impressed with the new recreational center you helped develop at Siedler Park. It's been a wonderful success, one which many other communities should look to for new ideas.

I'm writing to you because you are experienced in working with the elderly on recreational issues. During the past three years I've been completing my Master's degree in social work while teaching full-time at Wallace High School. I'm planning to leave teaching next year to pursue a career with community-based programs for the elderly.

My long-term career interests are in gerontology. While working on my Master's thesis—"Recreational Options for the Elderly: A Comparison of Three Innovative Community Programs"—I became very interested in working with local recreation programs. I'm now committed to pursuing a career relating to recreation and the elderly.

I would appreciate an opportunity to speak with you about your work in this field. At this stage I'm trying to learn as much as possible about career opportunities relating to recreation involving the elderly. Perhaps you could advise me on where and how I should best focus my job search during the next year.

I'll call your office next week to see if your schedule would permit a brief meeting to discuss my career interests. I would appreciate any information, advice, or tips you might provide me at this stage of my job search.

Sincerely,

Margaret Allen

## Cold Turkey
(possible opening)

5680 Citrine Blvd.
Pekin, IL 61559

March 1, 19____

John Dingle
General Manager
PEORIA GAZETTE
13 Walsh Street
Peoria, IL 61564

Dear Mr. Dingle:

I have five years experience as the Personnel Director at the Pekin Times. I have learned a great deal and contributed much during that time, and now would like to move to a position with a larger organization. While at the Times, I have learned specifically about personnel situations that are unique to the publishing business. It is for that reason that I would like to move to another news organization even though I realize that my personnel experience could be useful in many other businesses as well.

The Pekin Times has been leader in personnel innovations which have enabled me to put into place new policies which have been credited with increasing productivity and cutting costs while maintaining customer satisfaction. Highlights of my accomplishments include:

- Cost savings of 20% in medical premiums by instituting programs to improve employee health.

- Reduction of 18% in employee turnover by more carefully screening job applicants and training new employees.

- Reduction of 11% in employee absenteeism through a coordinated effort to respond to employee complaints by both Personnel and Department Managers.

I would appreciate the opportunity to talk with you about the directions you are headed at the Peoria Gazette. Whether or not we find that there might be an opportunity for me to work in your organization in the future, I think a meeting could be productive for both of us.

I will call you next week to schedule a meeting at your convenience.

Sincerely,

Jack Fielding

## Cold Turkey
(possible opening)

327 Saffron Court
Pensacola, Fl 33218

January 8, 19____

Darlene Textron
Editor
HONOLULU STAR BULLETIN
87 Lafayette Square
Honolulu, HI 96829

Dear Mrs. Textron:

For the past two years I have been a copywriter for the Pensacola News-Journal. I have found my time in this position to be both productive and enjoyable. I love writing for the newspaper!

I will be making a permanent move to Honolulu in early April and hope to continue to work in the news department for a major newspaper. I believe the Honolulu Star Bulletin would be a good fit for my interest and skills. As you can see from the resume I enclose, I was graduated from the University of Missouri with a double major in journalism and communication. The combination of my formal training with the excellent experience I have had at the Pensacola News-Journal have provided me with a solid background to become a contributing member of another news team. I have been fortunate here to have had the opportunity to work with and learn from some of the best newspeople in Florida. In fact, I was honored to be awarded the certificate of achievement as best copywriter in Northwest Florida at our regional meeting last month.

I will visit Honolulu early next month to make arrangements for housing and also plan to make contacts with various news organizations. I would like very much to talk with you about possible opportunities with the Honolulu Star Bulletin. I realize that you may not have a position open at present, but I believe it could be in the best interests of both of us to explore possible avenues that might be open in the future.

I will call you next week to see whether we might be able to meet briefly while I am in Honolulu. I will truly appreciate any time you could take from your busy schedule to meet with me. I feel sure I would benefit from having the opportunity to talk with you about the newspaper business in Hawaii.

Sincerely,

Phyllis Jourdan

## Cold Turkey
(information and advice)

4183 Waupelani Drive
State College, PA 16808

October 26, 19___

Dr. Harold Selnik
Chairman
Department of Speech Communication
UNIVERSITY OF PITTSBURGH
Pittsburgh, PA 12511

Dear Dr. Selnik:

I was fortunate to have been in the audience this past May when you gave the keynote speech at the Speech Communication Association Convention. Not only did your talk hold the entire audience spellbound, but I found your analysis of the future direction of our field to be the most insightful I have encountered.

I am completing the requirements for my Ph.D. in Communication at Penn State and will be graduated in May. I have not yet decided whether I would prefer to teach or use my background in Communication in another arena. Having heard you speak, I am certain your insights would be helpful to me as I consider this decision.

I will be in Pittsburgh over the Thanksgiving holiday. I hope that your schedule will permit you to meet briefly with me during that time. In fact, I could arrange my schedule to be in Pittsburgh a day before or after your holiday break at the University of Pittsburgh if that would be the most convenient for you.

I will call you next week. I hope we can schedule a meeting at a mutually convenient time. I value your opinions and feel certain that talking with you will enable me to better plan my future in Communication.

Sincerely,

Julie McGuire

## Referral
(information and advice)

4563 Southshore Drive
Key Biscayne, FL 33455

April 15, 19____

Marlo Sikes
Public Relations Director
DOLPHIN CRUISE LINE
873 North American Way
Miami, FL 33132

Dear Ms. Sikes:

Mr. Gerald Barnes of the Cruiseline Travel School, where I am a student, suggested I contact you for information regarding careers in the cruise industry. I will be completing my coursework here next month and am seeking information about opportunities in the travel industry in general and the cruiselines in particular. Mr. Barnes indicated you are one of the best sources of information as to the directions the cruise business is taking and that your network of persons involved in the business is the best of any around.

I realize your schedule is hectic, but I hope you will be able to help me by taking a half-hour of your time to meet with me to share your valuable information and insights into the cruise business with me.

I will call you next Monday to arrange a meeting at a time convenient for you. I truly will appreciate your assistance at this important juncture in plotting my future career.

Sincerely,

Miriam Jordan

## Referral
(possible opening)

9855 Little Glen Court
Dallas, TX 75207

June 23, 19___

Ida Stonewall
PACIFIC DESIGN CENTER
7008 Melrose Avenue
Los Angeles, CA 90069

Dear Ms. Stonewall:

A mutual friend of ours, Tina McGreggor at the Southwest Interior Design Center in Phoenix, suggested I write to you.

I have just completed the requirements for my M.B.A. degree from the University of Texas. As an undergraduate I had the opportunity to work as a co-operative education student in the administrative offices of the Dallas Design Center. I enjoyed my work there and want to explore the possibility of combining my business management training with my interest in design.

I will be returning to my family's home in Santa Monica next month. Tina indicated you would be one of the best people I could talk to regarding the kind of opportunities in the Los Angeles area for someone who was interested in work in one of the area design centers. She said your overview would help get me pointed in the right direction!

I will call you next week to see whether we could schedule a meeting during the week of July 10th. I would truly appreciate it if you could take time out from your busy schedule to meet with me.

Sincerely,

JoAnne McGrosney

## Referral
(possible opening)

485 High Bluff Road
Santa Fe, NM 89543

October 3, 19____

Rebecca Lyons
WESTERN INDUSTRIES, INC.
98347 W. Main Street
Albuquerque, NM 89977

Dear Mrs. Lyons:

Cynthia Pringle, my current supervisor and an acquaintance of yours, suggested I write to you. I will be relocating to Albuquerque within the next six weeks and will be looking for employment as a secretary. Cynthia indicated your firm is frequently in need of dependable and competent people to fill vacancies.

I have worked for Cynthia for the past three years and have consistently received "outstanding" ratings in all areas on my performance evaluations. I get along well with people and look forward to beginning work in a new firm in my new city.

I will be driving into Albuquerque the week of the 15th and hope I might be able to meet with you at that time. Even if you do not have a vacancy or anticipate one at this time, I would appreciate the opportunity to talk with you about other contacts I might make to further my job search in Albuquerque.

I will call you next week and hope we may be able to schedule a meeting. I will appreciate any assistance you may be able to give me and look forward to meeting you. Cynthia speaks so highly of you that I know your assistance would be truly valuable to me.

Sincerely,

Karen Jostney

## Referral
(possible opening)

650 Candlestick Lane
Orem, UT 80933

February 11, 19____

Jack Daniels
SUCCESS SEMINARS, INC.
19788 Expert Lane
Provo, UT 81566

Dear Mr. Daniels:

Jeff Holser, one of your former instructors, suggested that I contact you. He indicated that since your firm has been experiencing rapid growth, you would be a logical person for me to talk with regarding possible training opportunities with Success Seminars, Inc.

After teaching writing courses at Brigham Young University for eight years, I resigned to conduct training seminars for Write To The Point, Inc. and have been with them for the past three years. I like the travel opportunities involved in conducting training seminars across the country and enjoy working with the adult participants who enroll in their courses.

After twenty-five years offering training seminars, Write To The Point will be closing its doors since its owner is retiring from the business and has chosen to close rather than sell the business. Hence I am looking for opportunities to put my skills to work with another training firm. Jeff has spoken highly of your firm and the outstanding work that you do.

Some of my accomplishments with my present employer include:

- rated as "outstanding" instructor by 92% of seminar participants

- increased sales of audio tapes and books sold at seminars by over 50%

- 62% of participants who attend my seminars sign up for another seminar within six months

I would appreciate the opportunity to talk with you about your organization as well as possible ways we might work together. I will call you next Monday to schedule an appointment at a mutually convenient time. Thank you for your consideration.

Sincerely,

Bruce Italk

# Chapter Six

# RESPONDING TO VACANCY ANNOUNCEMENTS

If you are like many job seekers, you will spend much of your job search time responding to classified ads and job vacancy announcements with letters and resumes. While this approach may not be the most effective one for finding a job, nonetheless, it is one important approach that does lead to real jobs. Millions of jobs are announced in newspapers, magazines, and trade journals and posted on bulletin boards each year.

What type of letter will you write? What should it say about you in relation to the job vacancy? Will it represent your best writing effort? These and several other important questions are addressed in the sample letters appearing in this chapter.

## LETTERS REQUIRED

Job vacancy announcements come in many forms and include different types of instructions. Some may ask you to apply in person, which means you must complete an employer's application; you also may be interviewed at the same time. Other announcements may ask you to telephone for further information, which means you will experience a telephone screening interview prior to being contacted by an employer for a face-to-face interview. Others may ask you to send a resume and letter or complete an application. And still others may ask you to fax your resume. But most vacancy announcements require you to submit a letter and/or a resume.

Most responses to job vacancy announcements should include a letter. If you must submit a resume via the mail or by fax, be sure to include a cover letter. A resume submitted without an accompanying letter is likely to become a weak resume. The letter is analogous to a headline for advertising copy. It should be designed to grab attention and create interest in you and your resume. It enables you to express your personality, enthusiasm, and unique style—important hiring criteria which are difficult to express in a formal resume. It also should include the most important element in your job search at this stage—a follow-up statement specifying what action you will take next in reference to the letter recipient.

## TYPES OF LETTERS

Two basic types of letters are normally written in response to vacancy announcements:

- Cover letters

- Resume letters

**Cover letters** written in response to job vacancy announcements differ from other types of cover letters in one major respect—they respond to the specific requirements outlined in the vacancy announcement. As such, they do much more than merely provide cover for your resume. They focus your qualifications in reference to the needs of the employer. They tell employers that you have the necessary experience and qualifications as stated in the vacancy announcement as well as reflected in your resume.

**Resume letters** are letters of application which are not accompanied by a resume. When written in response to a vacancy announcement, a resume letter summarizes your qualifications in reference to the requirements outlined in the vacancy announcement. We examine the special case of resume letters in Chapter Eight.

## AUDIENCES

Job search letters written in response to vacancy announcements may or may not be addressed to a specific name or organization. In many cases an announcement will give the name of the person to whom an application letter and resume should be submitted. This contact name will enable you to include a follow-up statement in your letter. In other cases a classified ad only lists a postal box number or a mailing address minus an organizational or contact name. In these cases you do not know the identity of the organization nor its location. Letters responding to such anonymous ads will not include follow-up statements. They are least likely to receive a positive response—or any response at all. The letter examples in this chapter include responses to these different types of vacancy announcements.

## REMEMBER TO
## TAKE ACTION

If an ad or vacancy announcement reveals a contact name, address, or phone number, be sure to include a follow-up statement at the end of your letter. The reason most cover letters in response to vacancy announcements are ineffective has little or nothing to do with the contents or quality of the letter. Most are ineffective because the letter writer failed to take follow-up action in the form of a phone call.

---

*There is no such thing as a perfect or model cover letter that really works.*

---

The follow-up phone call is **the** key to making such cover letters effective. Without the phone call, your letter and resume joins an ocean of other similar resumes and letters. The follow-up statement alerts the letter recipient that he or she needs to read your resume and letter because you will be calling to inquire about your candidacy. This statement may also hasten a hiring decision—positive or negative.

If you send cover letters without such follow-up statements, or you fail to follow-up with a phone call, don't expect to hear from employers. If you want action on the part of the employer, then you must initiate the necessary action to ensure a response.

Again, there is no magic inherent in job search letters or resumes. Your written communication activities must be related to other equally important job search communication activities. There is no such thing as a perfect or model cover letter that really works.

The only thing that really works is you communicating directly with hiring officials. This occurs in the form of telephone or face-to-face interviews. Resumes and letters accompanied by a follow-up telephone call best get hiring officials to take action that gives positive direction to your job search.

## Consumer Advocate

**ROBBIN BARRETT**

221 Western Ave.                    Detroit, MI 47892                    919/231-3214

November 5, 19___

Katherine Kerry
Recruitment Director
CONSUMER UNION
29 Temple Place
Boston, MA 02111

Dear Ms. Kerry:

I read with interest your announcement for a Consumer Program Associate in the February issue of <u>Community Jobs</u>. This is an exciting position that should have a major impact on environmental and energy legislation.

As indicated in the enclosed resume, I believe my interests and background are ideally suited to this position. While completing my B.A. in communication, I promoted awareness of environmental and energy issues as a reporter for our campus newspaper. As a member of the Student Environmental Awareness Group, I helped organize conferences and successfully led demonstrations protesting the construction of a new library on the site of the campus arboretum. My involvement with such activities and issues convinced me to pursue an activist career relating to such public issues.

During the past three years I have been involved in all advocacy phases relating to consumer, environmental, and energy issues:

- lobbied state and local officials
- promoted consumer advocacy issues with campus groups and the media
- managed a citizen outreach office
- developed press materials and promotional strategies

Above all, I have a strong interest and commitment to these issues. I know how to work well with citizen groups, public officials, business groups, and the media.

I appreciate your consideration and look forward to discussing with you how I might best work with your organization. I'll call you next Wednesday to answer any questions you might have about my qualifications.

Sincerely,


Robbin Barrett

# Accounting Clerk

3713 Wilson Blvd.
Syracuse, NY 14992

May 2, 19___

SYRACUSE DAILY
Box M1108
Syracuse, NY 14992

I enclose a copy of my resume in reference to your announcement for an Accounting Clerk. With six years of progressive experience in accounting, I would bring to this position

- familiarity with AP/AR, billing, pricing, and cash receipts
- excellent typing (80 wpm) and filing skills
- knowledge of word processing, spreadsheet, and data base programs (WP5.1, Lotus, DBase IV)

While most of my experience is with personal computers, I am also familiar with a mainframe terminal.

I would appreciate an opportunity to interview for this position.

Sincerely,

Martha Ellis

## Director, Business Operations
(Health Care)

**STEVEN O'BRIEN**

7891 Donner Lane          Orlando, FL 35421          913/371-3981

July 5, 19___

Ms. Sharon Campbell
Director, Operations Support
DENVER GENERAL HOSPITAL
2033 Spring Road
Denver, CA 80023

Dear Ms. Campbell:

Your ad in yesterday's Denver Post for a Director of Business Operations attracted my attention for several reasons. I bring to this job

- 8 years of experience in healthcare finance with a 600+ bed acute care facility
- 5 years of progressively responsible reimbursement experience
- 3 years of management level experience in healthcare billing and collections
- familiarity with major computerized accounting and spreadsheet systems
- a solid record of accomplishment—increased collections by 47% and reduced accounting costs by 36% during the past two years as Assistant Director of Business Operations at Orlando General Hospital

I'm especially interested in moving to Denver where I spent my undergraduate years at the University of Denver. With family there, I already feel part of the community.

I enclose a copy of my resume as well as an article I recently completed on healthcare finance for your reference. The article summarizes much of my philosophy on healthcare finance approaches.

I'll call your office next Thursday afternoon to answer any questions you might have about my candidacy. I also have a few questions about the position.

Sincerely,

Steven O'Brien

## Criminal Justice

**MARCUS WELLINGTON, Ph.D.**

513 Annapolis Road          Annapolis, MD 24212          401/238-3192

January 7, 19___

Cheryl Grant
Personnel Director
Department of Public Safety
   and Correctional Services
6111 Reisterstown Rd., Suite 110
Baltimore, MD 21222-3142

Dear Ms. Grant:

I read with interest your vacancy announcement in the Sunday edition of The Baltimore Sun for Director, Division of Parole and Probation. As requested, I enclose a copy of my resume for your consideration.

I bring to this position nearly 10 years of progressive experience in the Maryland criminal justice system. After completing my B.A. in Criminal Justice from the University of Maryland, I worked as a police officer in Baltimore. I was especially fortunate to work alongside one of the city's leaders in correctional administration, R. Lance Donovan, who encouraged me to pursue a Master's degree in public administration with a specialty in correctional administration.

Since completing my graduate work 8 years ago, I've had a wonderful career in correctional administration. My work in the fields of parole and probation have convinced me of the importance of developing new approaches to correctional administration. During the past three years I've been involved in developing a model probation program that has reduced recidivism rates by nearly 30% within a two-year period. I'm excited about the opportunity this position would afford me to use my experience to further improve Maryland's parole and probation programs.

I would appreciate an opportunity to meet with you to discuss how my interests and qualifications can best meet your needs. I'll call your office next Wednesday to see if we might be able to meet at a mutually convenient time. I have several ideas I would like to share with you about how I might approach this position.

Sincerely,

Marcus Wellington

## Dispatcher

882 Forest Lane
Cleveland, OH 43210

March 1, 19____

P.O. Box 82
Cleveland, OH 43207

Here's my resume in response to your ad in today's <u>Cleveland Plain Dealer</u> for an evening dispatcher. I'm very familiar—nine years experience—with all aspects of trucking, warehouse, and communication operations. I worked as a driver for three years, a stevedore for two years, and an assistant warehouse manager for one year. During the past three years I've been an evening dispatcher with Bluebird Trucking. I have computer experience and I'm noted for working well with others in stressful settings.

I would appreciate more information on this position and your organization as well as an opportunity to interview for this position. Please give me a call if you need any additional information. You will find I have a pleasant telephone manner which is essential for a good dispatcher.

Sincerely,

Jack Diamond

# Editor

**MALISSA GROVES**

819 Elm Grove Circle          Boston, MA 02331          415/367-9220

August 17, 19____

Janet Akers
NATIONAL ASSOCIATION
 OF REALTORS
777 14th Street, NW
Washington, DC 20005

Dear Ms. Akers:

I'm submitting my resume and three writing samples in response to your announcement in today's <u>Washington Post</u> for an editor of the biweekly newspaper, <u>Realtor News</u>. I'm especially interested in this position because of my extensive reporting and editorial work on real estate. I would bring to this position

- six years of progressively responsible experience in reporting, writing, and editing
- extensive knowledge of the real estate industry
- an ability to meet tight deadlines
- an eagerness to work closely with fellow professionals

As indicated in my sample clippings, I've written and edited several lead articles on the real estate industry. I am also completing a book on today's changing real estate market which will be published next year. I believe I will bring to this position a solid record of writing and editing accomplishment.

I would appreciate an opportunity to discuss how my interests and qualifications can best meet your needs. I will call your office on Tuesday afternoon to answer any questions you might have about my candidacy.

Sincerely,

Malissa Groves

## Education

714 W. 42nd St.
Bremerton, WA 98213

October 21, 19___

Bruce Davidson
Department of Personnel/
   Human Resources
WALTON MIDDLE SCHOOL DISTRICT
401 McIntire Road
Seattle, WA 98111

Dear Mr. Davidson:

I enclose my resume in response to your announcement in today's <u>Seattle Times</u> for Principal of Walton Middle School. I would bring to this position

- 18 years of progressive experience in education, as both a classroom teacher and administrator

- a demonstrated record of teaching excellence, including teaching awards

- the ability to supervise teachers and classified staff

- a willingness to work closely with parents, teachers, and community leaders

I am currently completing my Ph.D. in educational administration with a specialty in elementary education.

Please let me know if you need any additional information. I will call you next Thursday morning to see if you have any questions about my candidacy. I would appreciate an opportunity to interview for this position.

Sincerely,

Tina Stewart

## Electronic Technician

4421 Sherman Avenue
Gainesville, FL 33412

May 29, 19____

James Thurber
ELECTRODYNE, INC.
8213 Bertram Road
Gainesville, FL 33410

Dear Mr. Thurber:

I enclose my resume in response to your announcement for a Field Service Technician or Technician Supervisor that appeared in today's Gainesville Sentinel. Based on the description, the positions appear ideally suited to my interests and skills.

I have a two year degree in electronics from the Electronics Institute. During the past three years I have worked as both a Field Service Technician and Technician Supervisor for Gainesville Cablevision. These jobs required excellent communication skills and trouble-shooting capabilities. My supervisor judged my performance to be "outstanding." Indeed, I was promoted to Technician Supervisor within 18 months.

Your ad requested salary history. When I started with Gainesville Cablevision I was making $21,500 a year. This year I am making $27,250 a year. I would expect this to increase to $28,350 by next year.

I would appreciate an opportunity to meet with you to discuss how my experience can best meet your needs. I will call you Wednesday afternoon to answer any questions you may have about my candidacy.

Sincerely,

Debra White

## Building Engineer

731 Ocean Breeze Dr.
Miami, FL 31114

February 7, 19___

Terry Barton
KEY MANAGEMENT CO.
7820 Ocean Blvd., Suite 131
Miami, FL 31110

Dear Mr. Barton:

I read with interest your ad in today's <u>Miami Herald</u> for a Building Engineer to handle a 130 unit condo project. I believe I have the necessary experience to do an excellent job. In addition, I am willing to live on the premises.

I have nearly seven years of experience as a Building Engineer. My experience involved

- working with all aspects of central heating plants
- diagnosing and resolving mechanical, electrical, and plumbing problems
- preparing equipment for inspections
- reporting monthly inspections to the condo association president and presenting an annual inspection report to association members

I pride myself in operating an effective preventive maintenance program which includes timely inspections and routine reporting procedures.

I would appreciate an opportunity to interview for this position. I'm especially interested in sharing with you a model preventive maintenance program I developed in my current job. It enabled the condo association to save over $100,000 a year in unnecessary repairs.

I'll call your office next Monday to see if you have any questions concerning my candidacy. I look forward to meeting you and learning more about the position.

Sincerely,

Samuel Rittenstone

## Environmental Engineer

717 N. Abbott St.
Amherst, MA 02432

March 22, 19____

Marilyn Reed
RTC TECHNOLOGY
188 Stevens Drive
St. Louis, MO 63211

Dear Ms. Reed:

I noticed with interest your announcement for an environmental engineer specializing in hazardous waste processing which was posted in the career office of the engineering department at the University of Massachusetts. I'm completing my Master's degree and will be available for full-time employment beginning in June.

I enclose my resume for your reference. During the past two years I have had an opportunity to both study and work in the environmental engineering field. My course work has focused on the engineering aspects of hazardous waste processing. During the past two summers I interned with one of the nation's largest environmental engineering firms, BTS Technology.

I would appreciate an opportunity to interview for this position. I will call your office Friday morning to see if you have any questions concerning my candidacy.

Sincerely,

Aaron Trisler

# Research Assistant

2714 East-West Highway
Washington, DC 20132

April 3, 19___

Rebecca Thomas
METROPOLITAN WASHINGTON
  COUNCIL OF GOVERNMENTS
777 No. Capitol St., NE, #101
Washington, DC 20002

Dear Ms. Thomas:

I'm very interested in the vacancy you advertised in today's Washington Post for a Research Assistant to study the region's solid waste management practices. I understand this position is for a 15-month period.

As a graduate with a B.S. in environmental science, I have conducted research relating to waste removal and management in the Washington, DC area while employed as a summer intern with R.C. Research Associates. My work involved surveying waste removal and recycling collection contracts, estimating waste generation rates, using computerized databases, and writing major sections of the final research report. I believe my research experience directly relates to the study for which you are recruiting a Research Assistant.

Please consider this letter and accompanying resume to be my application for this position. I'll call you on Monday afternoon to answer any questions you might have concerning my candidacy. I would be delighted to send you a copy of the final research report I helped complete on regional solid waste management.

Sincerely,

Gerald Edison

## Executive Secretary

**SHARON EVERS**

1324 Thomas Circle              Mobile, AL 35214              208/378-1392

November 5, 19____

Julian Woods
C. H. JAMISON ASSOCIATES
8714 Norton Avenue
Mobile, AL 35211

Dear Mr. Woods:

The Executive Secretary position you advertised in today's <u>Mobile Times</u> especially interests me. As the enclosed resume indicates, I have over seven years of secretary experience. During the past three years I've served as executive secretary to a financial investment firm of 85 employees. I regularly use WordPerfect 5.1 and Lotus and can quickly master other software programs as well as train employees.

You will also find that I am a dependable, loyal, and enthusiastic employee who works well under the pressure of deadlines. My previous employers gave me high marks for my administrative abilities in organizing office routines, handling travel schedules, communicating with departments, and organizing and planning meetings. I very much enjoy being Executive Secretary in a work environment that supports initiative and creativity.

I would appreciate an opportunity to interview for this position. I will call you Wednesday morning to see if you have any questions concerning my application.

Thank you for your consideration.

Sincerely,

Geraldine Wright

## Financial Analyst

**ROBIN ANSLER**

1061 Wilson Blvd.          Arlington, VA 23122          703/881-8291

January 30, 19___

Albert Jones
SPRINT INTERNATIONAL
12220 Sunrise Valley Drive
Reston, VA 22098

Dear Mr. Jones:

I know the importance of maintaining a sound financial analysis in the communication business. That's why I was attracted to your ad in the Washington Times for a Financial Analyst.

During the past four years I've worked in a similar position at MCI. We developed one of the most innovative financial reporting programs in the industry. It helped increase the profitability of MCI's International Voice Products by 22%.

I know your products and services well. Indeed, as MCI's major competitor for offshore customers, Sprint International has an excellent reputation for quality. It's the type of organization I find most attractive for the financial skills I possess. I believe we would work well together.

As indicated in the accompanying resume and in reference to the qualifications outlined in your ad, I have a BA in Accounting and an MBA in Finance. I regularly work with Lotus and Excel and exhibit strong oral and written communication skills.

I'll call your office Tuesday morning to see if you have any questions about my candidacy. I would appreciate an opportunity to discuss with you how my skills and experience can best meet Sprint's needs.

Sincerely,

Robin Ansler

## Grants Specialist

**ANDREW CLARK**
253 North Shore Dr.
Chicago, IL 60011
312/381-0812

February 18, 19____

Elizabeth Marlo, Ph.D.
Office of Faculty Development
UNIVERSITY OF ILLINOIS
One University Plaza
Chicago, IL 60015

Dear Dr. Marlo:

Can the University of Illinois use a Grants Specialist who can increase grants by 15% in a single year? That's what I've accomplished this past year as a Grants Specialist at Roosevelt University. This 15% increase translated into $4.2 million in additional grants awarded to the university. The resulting overhead increases enabled the university to create two new positions in Faculty Development.

I read with interest your announcement for a Grants Specialist in The Chronicle of Higher Education. As indicated in the accompanying resume, I have over eight years of grantsmanship experience in higher education. I've been involved in all phases of grants management, from developing and administering contracts, grants, and cooperative agreements with government agencies, corporations, and foundations to assisting faculty in developing proposal skills.

I would appreciate an opportunity to discuss how my qualifications can best meet your needs. I am especially interested in sharing with you a grantsmanship training program I developed at Roosevelt University for improving the capabilities of faculty to generate winning proposals.

I'll call your office Monday afternoon to answer any questions you may have about my qualifications. I look forward to meeting you.

Sincerely,

Andrew Clark

## Graphic Artist

**DEBRA SUMMERS**

781 Humphrey Blvd.          Minneapolis, MN 53821          812/928-0132

July 19, 19___

Sandra Delray
OLLEN GRAPHICS
182 Thompson Ave.
Suite 914
Minneapolis, MN 53824

Dear Ms. Delray:

The Graphic Artist position you advertised in today's <u>Minneapolis Times</u> fits me perfectly. I have the necessary motivation, skills, and experience to excel in this position.

I enclose a copy of my resume as well as a few samples of my work for your reference. These reflect a strong background in computerized graphic design. As indicated in your ad, you need someone who has expertise with Microsoft, Excel, and Pagemaker and who can do layout and paste up. I've worked with all of these programs and do layout and paste up on a daily basis.

I'll call you Wednesday morning to see if we might get together soon to discuss this position. I'm interested in learning more about your studio.

Sincerely,

Debra Summers

## Athletic Director

**LAURIE MAYNARD**

819 Switchback Road            Atlanta, GA 33913            291/309-3920

October 3, 19___

John Barnard
ATLANTA CLUB
918 Peachtree Ave.
Atlanta, GA 33919

Dear Mr. Barnard:

As the premier health club in Atlanta, I know how important it is to maintain a quality facility. And your club is one of the finest in the southeast. I know because I've visited many throughout the state as well as in Florida, South Carolina, Tennessee, and Alabama.

I'm especially interested in the Athletic Director position you advertised in today's Atlanta Constitution. As indicated in the accompanying resume, I have several years of experience as the Assistant Athletic Director at Atlanta Central High School. In addition, during the past two years, I have worked part-time as both an instructor and publicist at the Peachtree Health Club.

I believe I possess the necessary skills to do a first-class job as your Athletic Director. I helped plan, organize, and direct more than eight sports activities involving a student body of over 1,000. In addition, I was instrumental in developing a special athletic program for faculty and parents. I've made numerous presentations and know how to effectively market sports programs.

If you are looking for someone who takes initiative, can manage people, communicates well, knows how to market, and simply loves operating and developing sports programs, let's meet soon to discuss this position. I'll call you on Thursday afternoon to see if you have any questions about my candidacy. I have several ideas on how an Athletic Director with a background in education can best meet your needs.

Sincerely,

Laurie Maynard

## Health Education Evaluator

891 Wheeler Road
Charlotte, NC 34317

December 1, 19___

Ronald Rittenhouse, Director
Office of Human Resources
HEALTH RESOURCES, INC.
716 Sunnyside Avenue
Charlotte, NC 34317

Dear Mr. Rittenhouse:

I read with interest your ad in today's edition of the <u>Charlotte Times</u> for a Health Education Evaluator. As indicated in the accompanying resume and list of publications, I believe my background is ideally suited for this position.

I completed my MPH seven years ago at the University of North Carolina in Chapel Hill. Since then I have worked with the North Carolina Department of Health as a program analyst. After leaving the Department three years ago, I completed additional graduate work and did part-time evaluation research work with several health care firms. My reports have been well received by employers who regularly use me for part-time contract work.

I am interested in re-entering the health field on a full-time basis. As a former state employee involved in major health care policy issues and skilled in evaluation research, I believe I would bring to this position a unique blend of experience and skills that would prove invaluable to your organization. I am very familiar with the programs outlined in your ad and have expertise in the three program areas you mention—community program development, minority health education program development and implementation, and women's health issues.

We should meet to discuss how my background best fits into your hiring needs. I will call your office on Thursday morning to see if you have any questions as well as ask a few of my own. For example, are you familiar with the new NHC model which may soon be implemented at the state level? This is an area I'm very familiar with and which I believe has extremely important implications for minority health education programs and the contractors who deliver services to such programs.

Sincerely,

John Zigler

## Circulation Intern

712 W. Vermont St.
Washington, DC 20132

May 3, 19____

Elliott Stevens
WASHINGTON MONTHLY
1611 Connecticut Ave., NW
Washington, DC 20009

Dear Mr. Stevens:

While visiting the Department of Journalism at George Washington University today, I saw your announcement for a Summer Circulation Intern. I'm enclosing my resume as an application for this position.

I would really love working for the <u>Washington Monthly</u>. It's one of my favorite magazines. It maintains a unique muckraking tradition that is absent in much of today's print journalism. It would be exciting to play a role in increasing the circulation of your magazine.

I know my work experience in journalism is very limited. As a junior majoring in journalism, I've spent most of my time studying (18 hour semester course loads) while participating in some student activities. I'm taking off this summer to gain work experience relevant to my major. My long-term goal is to become an investigative reporter and then a manager of a newspaper or magazine.

While I don't have a great deal to offer you in terms of experience, I am a highly motivated, hard worker who wants to really learn the business from the bottom up. This internship will enable me to learn a great deal about promotion and distribution—areas which I have enjoyed the most in my journalism studies while also contributing to the promotion of my favorite magazine.

If you give me an opportunity to interview for this position, I promise you will not be disappointed. I'll call you on Friday morning to see if we might be able to meet to discuss the position.

Sincerely,

Tracey Nelson

# Cost Containment Coordinator

## DOROTHY HINES

9132 S. Wright St.                Providence, RI 01328                314/367-2874

June 14, 19____

Marilyn Deitz
THE HEALTH GROUP
7134 W. Madison
New Haven, CT 02814

Dear Ms. Deitz:

I read with interest your ad in this month's issue of <u>Healthcare Today</u> for a Cost Containment Coordinator. I am especially interested in this position because it is one of the most important for maintaining the financial viability of healthcare programs.

As indicated in the accompanying resume, I have an LPN and more than five years of experience in collecting, analyzing, and reporting healthcare cost and utilization data. I'm also skilled in the use of computer based data management systems and Lotus 1-2-3.

This position is ideally suited for my background and interests. I've previously worked for both an insurance company and a hospital and thus am very familiar with claims processing. I also played a major role in developing a hospital audit and physician review program at Providence Central Hospital.

Would you have a few minutes to speak with me about this position? I have a few ideas I would like to share with you on alternative ways to organize claims processing. I'll call you on Wednesday to check your schedule.

Sincerely,

Dorothy Hines

# Dispute Resolution Intake
# Coordinator

2908 Trail Drive
Atlanta, GA 32119

September 29, 19____

Barbara Haynes
Department of Dispute Resolution
SUPREME COURT OF GEORGIA
100 N. Eight Street, 2nd Floor
Atlanta, GA 32109

Dear Ms. Haynes:

I am enclosing my resume and the state application form you requested in response to the announcement for a Dispute Resolution Intake Coordinator for DeKalb County which appeared in last Sunday's <u>Atlanta Constitution</u>. I believe my interests and experience nicely coincide with the requirements for this position.

I have a Master's degree in Public Administration with a specialty in state court administration. As an undergraduate majoring in Criminal Justice, I worked two summers as a paralegal. As part of my graduate work, I interned with the state Office of Court Administration. There I became very familiar with the problems of an overloaded court system. Indeed, I was fortunate to work closely with a talented group of professionals who developed a pilot dispute referral and mediation program. I was especially delighted to learn their efforts were translated into what may well become a model program for other state court systems.

But what can I bring to this position that others may not? I am very familiar with your program. I'm experienced in

- screening and assessing court cases for possible referral to mediation
- conducting group orientations and individual assessments
- developing and maintaining lists of mediators
- evaluating program effectiveness
- developing criteria for case referral

I have worked closely with court administrators and community leaders in publicizing alternative programs for dispute resolution. I also have grantsmanship skills which should prove useful for this program.

I would appreciate an opportunity to interview for this position. I will call you Thursday morning to check on my application and to see if you have any questions concerning by background and skills.

Sincerely,

Kevin Anderson

### Rehab Nurse

**WANDA PETERS, RN**
213 Padra Fara, Apt. 137
Manila, The Philippines

June 23, 19____

Doris Silverman, MS, RN
Nurse Recruiter
OREGON GENERAL REHAB CENTER
8187 Elkins Drive
Portland, OR 98309

Dear Ms. Silverman:

Your ad in last week's <u>Portland Times</u> caught my mother's attention. She clipped the ad and faxed it to me in Manila.

After nearly 25 years of service with the U.S. Navy, I will be retiring this month. I will be returning to Portland within the next three weeks.

When I saw your ad, I was very pleased to learn it was for a rehab nursing position in Portland. The skills and experience you outline for this position are exactly the ones I possess. During the past eight years I worked as part of a rehab team at three Naval health facilities—Washington, DC, Hawaii, and Subic Bay. I've worked closely with medical professionals, patients, and their families.

Please look over the enclosed resume and let me know if you need any additional information. My international fax number is 011-82-283-292. After July 15, I can be contacted directly in Portland: 178 W. Terrace, Portland, OR 98311, Tel. 717/891-3291.

I look forward to meeting with you to discuss how my skills and experience can best meet the needs of Oregon General Rehab Center.

Sincerely,

Wanda Peters, RN

## Occupational Therapist

717 Georgia Avenue
Indianapolis, IN 48712

March 1, 19___

Barry Bates
Human Resources
GREATER INDIANAPOLIS HOSPITAL
67100 Conners Road
Indianapolis, IN 48712

Dear Mr. Bates:

Please consider the accompanying resume an application for the Occupational Therapist position you advertised in today's <u>Indianapolis Journal</u>.

As a recent graduate and licensed therapist, I believe I am well qualified for this entry-level position. Prior to completing my degree and becoming licensed, I worked as a paramedic and volunteer health worker. Confronting numerous trauma cases involving auto accidents, I decided I really wanted to work on rehab and acute care cases in a hospital setting. Completing the degree and becoming a licensed therapist is a dream come true.

I would appreciate an opportunity to interview for this position. The acute care unit at Greater Indianapolis General Hospital has a well deserved reputation for excellent patient care. I know since I visited there numerous times with patients. I would be proud to join in contributing to the team effort.

I will call you on Friday morning to see if you have any questions about my candidacy. I look forward to meeting with you and your staff.

Sincerely,

Susan Wright

## Office Manager/Bookkeeper

1801 Morton Lane
Detroit, MI 48723

September 23, 19___

FAXED TO: 319/393-2984

I read with interest your ad in today's <u>Detroit Sun</u> for an Office Manager/
Bookkeeper. The accompanying resume summarizes my experience relevant to
the qualifications you outlined.

Please note that I have served as both an office manager and bookkeeper for
more than 12 years. Most of my experience is with the printing industry. I
have supervised a staff of eight, performed general ledger functions, and am
experienced in using Lotus 1-2-3. I love working with details, and I consistently meet my deadlines.

Since your ad did not include a company name nor address, I would appreciate it if you could give me more information about your organization and its
location. The ad mentioned a printing company. I assume you are located in
the Detroit area since we are in the same area code to which I am faxing this
letter and resume.

I look forward to learning more about your company.

Sincerely,

Donald Reid
Fax 319/281-3192

## Paralegal

241 West Laramie
Albany, NY 14988

October 2, 19____

Box M1230
ALBANY RECORD
Albany, NY 14992-1283

Your ad in today's newspaper caught my attention because it specified
someone with FCC experience and a student who might be attending law
school at night. As the accompanying resume indicates, my interests, experience, and schedule may be ideally suited to your needs.

My FCC experience was acquired during the past two years while working
in Washington, DC on Capitol Hill as a Legislative Aid to Representative
Wilson. I was responsible for developing legislative proposals relevant to FCC
operations. In the process of doing this work I became very familiar with the
day-to-day operations of the FCC. Many of my FCC contacts are still in place.

When Representative Wilson unexpectedly lost his bid for re-election, I
immediately returned to Albany. I decided to study law at the University of
Albany and enrolled as an evening student. My long-term plans are to pursue a
law career in the Albany area.

I would appreciate an opportunity to interview for this position. I believe
you will find my Capitol Hill and FCC experience to be a real plus in working
with your firm.

Sincerely,

Harold Stevenson

## Optometric Assistant

197 Memphis Road
Knoxville, TN 38239

September 12, 19____

Dr. Winston Solane
SOLANE OPTICAL CO.
712 W. Memphis Ave.
Knoxville, TN 38241

Dear Dr. Winston:

According to your ad in today's <u>Knoxville Times</u>, you are looking for someone to assist a Visual Therapist. As requested, I enclose a copy of my resume for your reference.

I have two years of optical experience as both a frame stylist and an assistant to a Visual Therapist. I am familiar with most aspects of an optical business and I work well with customers. I worked extremely well with the Visual Therapist when I was employed at Westview Optical Company. Please feel free to contact my previous employer (John Steffle, Tel. 389-2899) who found me to be exceptionally cooperative and who frequently received positive feedback from his customers about my work.

Your ad also requested salary requirements. I'm unable to give you a figure at this time. My salary requirements are flexible, depending on the nature of the work and responsibilities. I really need to know more about the position and your company before I can respond to salary considerations.

I look forward to learning more about this position and how my skills can best meet your needs.

Sincerely,

Jodie Murphy

## Parks and Recreation Director

## SYLVIA WHITEHURST

8712 Graham Blvd.          Staunton, VA 23212          703/183-2314

January 14, 19___

Edward Jason
Personnel Administration
CITY OF CHARLESTON
P.O. Box 2918
Charleston, WV 25331

Dear Mr. Jason:

I read with interest your ad in the <u>Washington Post</u> for a Parks and Recreation Director. I am especially interested in this position because I have held a similar position here in Virginia. Having accomplished my goals in my present position, I'm now looking for another challenge in the parks and recreation field.

As indicated on the accompanying resume, I have a Master's degree in Parks and Recreation, two years experience as Assistant City Manager, and four years experience as the Parks and Recreation Director in Staunton, Virginia. As Director, I

- directed all phases of community recreational programs and public grounds
- supervised a staff of 26
- prepared and administered a $1.2 million annual budget

I have very much enjoyed my work in Staunton. I have a solid record of accomplishment. Since I took over as the Parks and Recreation Director, public use of public recreational facilities has increased by 45%. We have been able to meet increased demands with only a 15% increase in the parks and recreation budget. We have done this through an innovative volunteer instructional program that has eliminated the need for additional staff to operate summer recreational programs.

I would appreciate an opportunity to interview for this position. I will call your office on Tuesday afternoon to see if your schedule would permit us to meet. Since I will be visiting Charleston during the week of January 24, perhaps we could meet at that time.

Sincerely,


Sylvia Whitehurst

## Parts Manager

8149 Superior Ave.
Duluth, MN 50139

March 2, 19___

Lee Fuller
POWER RENTAL CO.
718 W. 24th St.
Duluth, MN 51039

Dear Mr. Fuller:

Please accept the enclosed resume as my application in response to your ad in today's <u>Duluth Times</u> for a Parts Manager. You stated you needed an experienced manager who has worked with large equipment and who is familiar with ordering inventory and managing personnel.

I believe I have the necessary experience and skills to do this job well. During the past 15 years I have worked at all levels and in a variety of positions in the parts business. I began in receiving, moved on to manage a stock room, took customer orders, and managed a parts warehouse with 13 employees. I'm experienced in operating computerized inventory systems. In my current job I decreased warehouse labor costs by 35% by installing a new inventory system.

I would appreciate the opportunity to interview for this position. Please expect a phone call from me on Thursday afternoon. I'll be calling for more information about the position as well as to answer any questions you may have about my candidacy.

Sincerely,


Vick Russell

## Pension Plan Administrator

### ELIZABETH CARSON

813 S. 9th St.   Columbus, MO 62351   819/231-3091

November 3, 19____

Bernard Graham
B. C. SYSTEMS, INC.
3819 Industrial Place
Columbus, MO 62350

Dear Mr. Graham:

I learned about your vacancy for a Pension Plan Administrator in this month's issue of JobMarket. As requested, I enclose a copy of my resume for your reference.

I have seven years of "hands on" experience as a Pension Plan Administrator. I am knowledgeable in pension law and regulations and experienced in handling defined contribution and defined benefit plans. My responsibilities have included checking, participant recordkeeping, 550 preparation, and client contact. I also have a CPA.

You may be interested in the new automated pension plan system I was instrumental in developing for my present employer. It reduced administrative costs by nearly 30% within the first two years of operation.

Please let me know if you need any additional information. I will call your office on Monday afternoon to see if you have questions about my candidacy.

Sincerely,

Elizabeth Carson

## Human Resources Analyst

**JANET ENGLE**
241 Marlboro Lane
Raleigh, NC 27210
717/894-2281

March 11, 19___

Gloria Manns
CHARLOTTE-MECKLENBURG SCHOOLS
P.O. Box 30154
Charlotte, NC 28241

Dear Ms. Manns:

Your recent ad in <u>School Administrator</u> for a Human Resources Analyst interests me for several reasons. I have the necessary qualifications you outlined for this position. I'm very attracted to the Charlotte area. And I believe this is a position in which I would excel.

I would bring to this position several important qualifications and experiences acquired during my 15 years of work in education:

- Master's degree in Psychology
- experience in job evaluation, benefits administration, compensation analysis, performance design, and quality intervention
- microcomputer proficiency
- knowledge of performance measurement and design models

I would appreciate an opportunity to interview for this position. Please expect a call from me Thursday afternoon. I have a few questions concerning this position. Perhaps you also may have questions about my candidacy.

Sincerely,

Janet Engle

### Hotel—Guest Services
### Manager

## WAYNE STEINBERG

5491 Mountain View Dr.      Sacramento, CA 95421            219/729-2912

July 8, 19____

Martha Albertson
Personnel Department
HOLIDAY INN NATIONAL
319 Granite Stone Dr.
San Diego, CA 92351

Dear Ms. Albertson:

Your ad in today's <u>San Diego Times</u> for a Guest Services Manager caught my attention. Therefore, I'm submitting my resume as an application for this position.

I believe I have the necessary experience to manage guest services for your 300 room hotel. My experience includes:

- three years supervisory experience—both AM and PM shifts
- strong rate management skills
- cost controls of payroll and expenses
- training guest relations personnel

I also have received extensive training in night audit.

I would appreciate an opportunity to interview for this position. I'll call your office on Tuesday afternoon to answer any questions you may have about my candidacy.

Sincerely,


Wayne Steinberg

### Healthcare—Clinical
### Data Analyst

**STEPHANIE OLSON**
382 Winter Green Dr.
Philadelphia, PA 17923
216/378-2981

October 9, 19____

David Maris
KAISER PERMANENTE
P.O. Box 9884
Philadelphia, PA 17929

Dear Mr. Maris:

Your ad in today's <u>Philadelphia Inquirer</u> for a Clinical Data Analyst caught my attention. I have a Master's degree in Public Health and four years experience as an analyst providing technical support for quality assurance. I especially enjoy working with statistical analysis.

As indicated in the accompanying resume, my experience includes the skills you require—developed and maintained computerized databases for peer review, quality screen, and clinical studies. In addition, I am very familiar with personal computers and database management in healthcare. This includes knowledge and experience in Paradox, DB Graphics, RBase, and DBase III+.

I would appreciate an opportunity to interview for this position. I will call your office on Tuesday afternoon to see if you have any questions about my candidacy.

Sincerely,

Stephanie Olson

## Information Services Librarian

**JULIE STROOMER**

179 W. 27th St.          San Francisco, CA 94131          419/384-2093

August 25, 19____

Betsy Kramer
AMERICAN SCHOOL BOARDS
  ASSOCIATION
2792 Hillcrest Dr.
San Francisco, CA 94123

Dear Ms. Kramer:

My 10 years of experience as an Information Services Librarian appears to be ideally suited for the position you advertised in this month's issue of <u>America's Schools</u>. You need someone who can

- oversee the activities of your organization's information services, resource center, and clearinghouses
- provide staff and constituents with information when needed
- manage day-to-day communications operations
- supervise a group of five employees
- demonstrate strong oral and written communication skills

As indicated on my enclosed resume, I acquired this experience over a 15 year period as the Information Services Librarian for U.S. Department of Interior's regional library service and as a high school librarian.

I also meet the qualifications you specify for this position. I have a Master's degree in Library Science with an emphasis on managing library information systems. Since I have worked closely with secondary and elementary schools, I am very knowledgeable about education and school governance issues as well as information and reference sources in education. During the past five years I supervised eight employees.

I would appreciate an opportunity to meet with you to discuss how my experience and qualifications can best meet your needs. I have additional skills which you might find useful for this particular position. I will call you on Wednesday morning to answer any questions you may have concerning my candidacy.

Sincerely,

Julie Stroomer

## Information Systems Specialist

231 Westview Terrace
Benton Harbor, MI 48270

February 27, 19____

Eric Nelson
NCCR, INC.
1900 North Echos Road
Benton Harbor, MI 48271

Dear Mr. Nelson:

I read with interest your ad in the <u>Benton Harbor</u> times for an Information Systems Specialist. As the accompanying resume indicates, I have the requisite skills and experience you outlined for this position. My 12 years with the U.S. Navy has prepared me well in the use of numerous computer systems and languages.

You may also be interested in several additional skills I would bring to this position:

- designed, coded, and tested network application software
- proficient in several high level computer languages ("C", etc.) and operating systems (UNIX, DOS) and windowing systems (X-Windows)
- planned systems management for communications network
- conducted research and development work on systems management and network simulation

I would appreciate an opportunity to interview for this position. I will call you on Thursday morning to answer any questions you may have concerning my candidacy.

Sincerely,

Debra Winston

## Insurance Casualty
## Claim Adjuster

1103 Wilson Blvd.
Buffalo, NY 14830

March 8, 19___

Sharon Drews
SILVAN CORPORATION
913 Benton Road
Buffalo, NY 14832

Dear Ms. Drews:

I enclose my resume in response to your ad in today's <u>Buffalo Evening Star</u> for a Casualty Claims Adjustor. This position is ideally suited for my skills and experience.

I have a Bachelor's degree in Business and five years of progressively responsible experience handling worker's compensation and general liability claims. During the past two years I have been responsible for developing an innovative casualty claims system for the American Insurance Company. I believe my work with this system may be of interest to Silvan Corporation.

Please let me know if you need any additional information to complete my application. I'll call you on Tuesday afternoon to answer any questions you may have about my candidacy.

Sincerely,

Beth Clarion

## Interior Design/Sales

1093 Martin Falls Rd.
Newark, NJ 07194

April 4, 19___

Box M118
NEWARK DAILY
Newark, NJ 07192

Are you looking for someone who can increase your sales by 50% within six months? If so, you need not look further. During my first six months as a sales associate for C. Irwin Interiors, I increased sales furniture and furnishings/ accessories by 50%. More importantly, this translated into $650,000 in additional commercial business. Since then, I've remained one of the company's top performers.

I enclose my resume in response to your ad in today's newspaper for an Interior Design/Sales position. We should meet soon to discuss how my experience and approach to interior design sales can best benefit your firm.

I look forward to hearing from you.

Sincerely,

Brenda Faris

## International Development

**LYNNE GARDNER**

8172 Western Ave.        Cedar Rapids, IA 54019        412/382-1333

August 17, 19____

Morris Edelson
Recruitment Committee
ICRW INTERNATIONAL
28 W. 32nd Street
New York, NY 10031

Dear Mr. Edelson:

Your ad in this week's issue of the International Employment Gazette for a social scientist to work on international development issues struck my attention for several reasons:

- I have over 12 years of experience in international development—seven involving residence abroad as a Peace Corps Volunteer, student, and contractor/consultant

- I have the policy relevant experience you require—completed my Ph.D. dissertation on women in development issues as well as conducted three consulting projects on family planning policy in Asia and Africa.

- I have contract administration and supervisory experience at the field level.

- I am prepared to relocate abroad for a two to three year project period.

I would very much appreciate an opportunity to interview for this position. I will call your office on Friday morning to answer any questions you may have about my previous work and how my experience and skills could best ensure a successful project for ICRW International.

Sincerely,

Lynne Gardner

# Laboratory Technician

116 Grandview Road
Dallas, TX 78217

May 23, 19___

Jedd Jamison
Human Resources
LATIMORE LABORATORIES
P.O. Box 138
Dallas, TX 78213

Dear Mr. Jamison:

I enclose my resume in response to your ad in today's <u>Dallas Star</u> for a Laboratory Technician. My educational background, knowledge, and experience appear to perfectly match the requirements you outlined for this job.

I have a B.S. in Biology from North Texas State University. During the past three years I have been employed by Douglas Laboratories in its DNA products laboratory. I regularly work with DNA sequencing, plamid purification, and recombinant techniques.

You requested that salary requirements accompany the resume. My requirements are flexible at this time. My current salary is $33,500—about average for an entry-level position plus three years experience in this field. While I would expect a salary commensurate with my level of experience, I need to know more about the position and your organization before I can give you a figure.

I would appreciate an opportunity to discuss this position with you. I will call you on Tuesday afternoon to answer any questions you may have about my candidacy.

Sincerely,

Gerry Gray

# Landscape Architect

**MARILYN JACOBS**
4215 Florida Ave.
Orlando, FL 31483
309/318-2851


James O'Brien
NEW MARKET FARMS
131 Market St.
Orlando, FL 31486


Dear Mr. O'Brien:

As requested in your announcement in today's <u>Orlando Times</u> for a Landscape Architect, I'm enclosing my resume and a sample of my work. I have a BSLA and two years of design experience primarily working on large commercial projects.

I'm especially interested in this position because your firm has an excellent reputation for doing some of the most creative and innovative commercial landscape work in the Orlando area. It's the type of firm I would be pleased to join.

I would appreciate an opportunity to interview for this position as well as share with you more examples of my work. I am noted for combining arid Southern California styles with more tropical Florida styles. My work has been well received by my present employer who regularly receives praise from satisfied clients.

I will call you on Wednesday morning to answer any questions you may have about my application.


                                              Sincerely,



                                              Marilyn Jacobs

## Legal Secretary

7172 Whispering Willow Rd.
Columbus, OH 45183

June 4, 19____

Thomas Pickering
DIAMOND, ESTER, AND GRACE
718 Jason Avenue
Columbus, OH 45183

Dear Mr. Pickering:

I'm responding to your ad that appeared in Sunday's <u>Columbus Dispatch</u> for a legal secretary. I have seven years of experience working for a mid-size law firm specializing in patent law. I would bring to this position the following experience and skills:

- ability to both type and take shorthand at 80+ wpm
- familiarity with WordPerfect 5.1
- excellent spelling and grammar skills
- energy, enthusiasm, and the ability to work on my own

I am used to working under deadlines and I am willing to work overtime to get the job done.

Your ad also mentioned salary requirements. My current salary is $31,500 per year with full benefits. Given my level of experience as well as current salary ranges for legal secretaries in patent law, I would expect to be offered this position in the $33,000 to $35,000 range, depending on the requirements of the job.

Please let me know if you need any additional information. I'll call you on Tuesday afternoon to answer any questions you may have concerning my candidacy.

Sincerely,

Margo Redding

## Legislative Assistant

**MICHAEL SHIELDS**
313 Wyoming Avenue
Washington, DC 20018
202/718-8291

June 19, 19____

Margaret Ballantine
FIELD, STERLING, AND JAMES
1191 Connecticut Ave., NW
Suite 918
Washington, DC 20036

Dear Ms. Ballantine:

After working on Capitol Hill for three years as a Legislative Assistant to two members of Congress, I'm interested in doing similar work with a government relations firm. That's why your ad in today's Washington Post caught my attention.

The accompanying resume summarizes my experience on Capitol Hill. As a Legislative Assistant, I specialized in tax and health issues which are the policy areas you mentioned in your ad. I've worked closely with the relevant congressional committee staffs, government agencies, and representatives of industry concerned with these two issues. I believe you will find I have the necessary knowledge and contacts to become a productive member of your team.

Your ad also mentioned MacIntosh experience. I am familiar with both MacIntosh and IBM systems. I also am familiar with Pagemaker and Ventura desktop publishing systems.

I'll call your office on Thursday morning to answer any questions you may have about my candidacy.

I look forward to sharing my legislative experience on tax and health issues with you in the very near future.

Sincerely,

Michael Shields

## Management

**GERALD DALTON**

818 Canyon Road          Riverside, CA 91483          819/290-1982

July 19, 19___

Marc Kaiser
RENT-A-CENTER
9128 Thompson Road
Los Angeles, CA 91589

Dear Mr. Kaiser:

In response to your ad in today's <u>Los Angeles Times</u>, I am enclosing my resume in application for the management opportunities you outlined. I understand you are willing to train individuals for these positions.

My background appears to be ideally suited for this opportunity. I have a Bachelor's degree in Accounting. I previously acquired management experience while working in a restaurant and managing a small retail furniture store. From both experiences I learned the importance of maintaining excellent customer relations and operating an efficient collections system—two skill areas you mentioned as important to the management opportunities.

Please expect to hear from me Friday morning. I will call your office to answer any questions you may have about my candidacy.

Sincerely,

Gerald Dalton

## Management/Store Manager

**ALICE WALKER**
192 West Norton Ave.
Pittsburgh, PA 18291
719/381-9471

January 6, 19___

Albert Black
Personnel Department
THE SOUTHLAND CORPORATION
9103 McNeil Street
Philadelphia, PA 17891

Dear Mr. Black:

I read with interest your ad in today's <u>Pittsburgh Times</u> for an experienced Store Manager with good interpersonal skills and three years previous management experience.

As indicated in the accompanying resume, I have the exact skills and experience you require. During the past seven years I have

- managed both a restaurant and retail video store—I know how important good customer relations are to the success of a business!

- supervised up to 12 employees

- made tough hiring and firing decisions

- experienced both the failure and success of two businesses—the restaurant was a victim of arson but the video store was a phenomenal success—increasing annual rentals/sales by 40%

We should talk soon about this position. I'll call you on Friday morning to answer any questions you may have about my candidacy.

Sincerely,

Alice Walker

## Management

8004 Elk Grove Dr.
Columbia, SC 32812

November 5, 19___

Box 918
COLUMBIA DISPATCH
Columbia, SC 32812

I read with interest this brief ad that appeared in last Sunday's edition of the Columbia Dispatch:

> MANAGEMENT - Will train aggressive individuals to top
> level management and six figure income. Rapid advancement
> to $50K.

Of course, like many others who contact you, I'm interested. I am aggressive but not to the point of being overbearing.

The enclosed resume summarizes my management experience. I have a strong pattern of management success, regardless of whom I work for or the type of organization, product, or service involved.

If I am the type of person you think would be a valuable addition to your operations, then let's talk soon about how we might best work together.

Sincerely,


Martin Throel

## Manager Trainee

334 Winthrop Street
Oak Lawn, IL 60331

July 21, 19____

Box 183
CHICAGO TRIBUNE
183 Michigan Avenue
Chicago, IL 60001

I read with interest your ad in today's <u>Chicago Tribune</u> for college grads interested in a management career with a national company.

As my accompanying resume indicates, I graduated from the University of Illinois in June. I majored in political science and minored in accounting.

I am interested in pursuing a long-term management career with a major national company. While working my way through college, I initially became a waiter and was later promoted to assistant manager of a restaurant. I very much enjoyed my management experience, especially supervising employees and maintaining accurate accounts. I believe this experience as well as my undergraduate studies have prepared me well for a career in management.

I would appreciate an opportunity to interview for this position. I believe you will find I have the necessary prerequisites to excel as a management trainee.

Sincerely,

Gary Turner

### Management/Store

3801 Walnut Street
Los Angeles, CA 91080

September 11, 19___

Jennifer Strong
THE GREEN BEAN CO.
241 Greenbrier Road
Los Angeles, CA 91093

Dear Ms. Strong:

I was delighted to learn in today's <u>Milwaukee Journal</u> that you will be opening three branch stores in the Milwaukee area. You have wonderful products which I regularly purchase through your mail order catalog.

But now to discover you are looking for managers of these stores is even more exciting. I want to throw my hat in the ring and let you know why you should interview me for one of these positions.

I enclose my resume for your reference. Please note that I have three years of management experience with Healthy Harvest Heaven. I served as assistant manager until the store closed in March of last year. Unfortunately, the owners decided to close the business and move to Florida. It was a very successful store that left many disappointed customers who will undoubtedly turn to your stores in the very near future.

I believe my management experience and enthusiasm for your products make a winning combination. I'll call you Monday, September 19, to answer any questions you may have about my candidacy.

Sincerely,

Linda Perry

# Market Analyst

918 Western Blvd.
Kansas City, KS 47831

March 21, 19___

Martin Jamison
HEALTHCARE ASSOCIATES
9981 Jefferson Highway
Suite 903
Las Vegas, NV 89312

Dear Mr. Jamison:

I just received this month's issue of <u>Healthcare News</u> and noticed your ad for a Market Analyst with consulting experience.

I believe I have the skills and experience you need. In addition to a Master's Degree in Public Health, I have four years experience as a Market Analyst in the healthcare field. During this time I have conducted over 10 major research projects which involved gathering and analyzing data, writing reports, and presenting findings to funding agencies. I always meet my deadlines and produce first-class products which are well received by sponsors. I am knowledgeable in the use of the two computer programs you mentioned in your ad—WIN 3.1 and EXCEL.

I would be happy to send you a sample of my work, especially a recent report I completed on the comparative costs of alternative healthcare markets for the U.S. Department of Health and Human Services.

I'll call you next Thursday afternoon to answer any questions you may have about my candidacy.

Sincerely,

George Barton

## Marketing/Art

**BEVERLY SIMON**

29 Little Run Road          Boston, MA 02193          918/382-4510

December 29, 19___

Kerry Klein
INTERNATIONAL ART EXPRESS
792 New England Avenue
Boston, MA 02193

Dear Mr. Klein:

What a wonderful position for someone with an art and marketing background! Your ad in today's <u>Boston Globe</u> for a self-starter to market your Art Leasing programs really caught my attention and immediately sent me to my word processor. It appears perfectly tailored to by interests, skills, and experience. It's as if I had written it for myself.

We really should meet to discuss how I would handle this position. I believe it is the perfect fit for me since the position combines my two loves—art and marketing.

Indeed, I have prepared well for this position. I have a Bachelor's degree in Art History and a Master's degree in Marketing. In addition, I have worked in two art galleries as the person in charge of sales and marketing. In both cases I was successful in increasing sales by 30% over an 18 month period. Most of this increase was due to my innovative and aggressive approach to the corporate market. I also introduced a successful corporate leasing program which now constitutes 35% of these galleries' revenues.

I will call your office on Friday morning to answer any questions you may have about my candidacy.

Sincerely,

Beverly Simon

## Marketing/Senior Project
## Manager


**GRANT OLIVER**
7119 W. Morgan Ave.
Louisville, KY 41313
209/781-9301


August 21, 19____


Margaret Harrison
SIMON AND JORDAN
381 Warner Drive
Suite 109
Louisville, KY 41319


Dear Ms. Harrison

Your ad in today's <u>Louisville Journal</u> for a Senior Project Coordinator for direct mail and other marketing projects interests me for several reasons. I have the requisite skills and experience specified in your announcement. I know the direct mail market well. And I have over five years of experience in both direct mail and insurance marketing.

Since graduating with a BA in communication eight years ago, I have acquired progressively responsible experience in the direct mail and advertising fields. I have strong copy writing skills that are best represented in the enclosed samples of my work. I also enjoy working with details, I am especially knowledgeable about demographics and list selection, and manage to juggle a variety of activities to meet deadlines.

Please consider the accompanying resume and work samples to be an application for this position. I will call you on Wednesday morning to answer any questions you may have about my candidacy.


Sincerely,


Grant Oliver

## Meeting Planner

811 Weston Road
Detroit, MI 48123

June 5, 19___

Leslie Bailey
Catering Manager
V.I.P. CLUB
491 Main Street
Detroit, MI 48130

Dear Ms. Bailey:

I enclose my resume in response to your ad in the <u>Detroit Sun</u> for a Meeting Planner. As the largest private club in Detroit, your reputation as one of the area's finest operations with large meeting facilities is well deserved. I know this is a very important position for your organization.

During the past three years I have worked as an Assistant Meeting Planner with the Detroit Convention Center. My work involved booking banquet groups, contacting clients, and marketing meeting services. I really enjoy this type of work, especially the details of getting groups scheduled and organized for events and solving problems of clients.

I would appreciate an opportunity to interview for this position. I plan to call your office on Friday morning to answer any questions you may have about my application for this position.

Sincerely,

Robert Gillian

## Mortgage Banking/
## Loan Officer

4219 Gadwell Place
Virginia Beach, VA 23492

September 16, 19____

Jeffrey Allen
JEFFERSON MORTGAGE COMPANY
1873 Granby Street
Norfolk, VA 23500

Dear Mr. Allen:

As a Loan Officer at Commonwealth Bank, I originated more loans than any other employee in the past five years. That's why I think we should discuss the position you advertised in today's Norfolk Ledger-Star.

I enclose a resume which you requested. If you will give me a few minutes of your time, I believe it will be more than worth your while. I'll share with you one of my best kept secrets as to why I will most likely become a top performer at Jefferson Mortgage Company, too.

I'll call your office next Wednesday to see if you are interested in getting together to discuss my role at Jefferson Mortgage Company.

Sincerely,

Wanda Wright

## Nurse Practitioner

8115 West 11th St.
Evanston, IL 60012

August 11, 19____

Betty Clarke, RN
Nurse Recruiter
THE NEUROLOGY CENTER
27 Sheridan Road
Evanston, IL 60015

Dear Ms. Clarke:

The accompanying resume is in response to your ad in today's <u>Chicago Sun Times</u> for a Nurse Practitioner. Given my past training, experience, and professional interests, this is the type of challenging position I most enjoy.

During the past five years I have worked as a Nurse Practitioner in the neurological unit of Evanston General Hospital. I was responsible for direct patient care with an emphasis on patient teaching and family/community education. I also helped develop the bladder and bowel management program at Evanston General. I believe you are planning to develop a similar program at your Center.

I am interested in continuing my career with a large private neurological practice. Your organization has an outstanding reputation as a one of the country's foremost neurological programs. I would like to contribute to the work of such a professional team.

I will call you on Thursday morning to answer any questions you may have concerning my application.

Sincerely,

Valerie Young

## Travel Consultant

**DARRELL BAIRD**
234 Wayfare Road
Madison, WI 53123,
317/382-9831

4912 Planter Place
Madison, WI 53122

May 19, 19____

Marlene Powers
Personnel Department
XSELL WORLD TRAVEL
391 Capitol Street
Madison, WI 53122

Dear Ms. Powers:

I have five years of experience as a travel agent. During the past two years I worked mainly with corporate clients.

Your ad in today's <u>Madison Times</u> for a Travel Consultant appears to fit nicely with my interests, skills, and experience. As indicated in the accompanying resume, I am an Apollo/Focal Point agent with ADS computer experience. Since many of my clients travel abroad, I have extensive experience in international travel operations. My previous employers praised my excellent telephone manner and my ability to take charge in stressful situations.

I would appreciate the opportunity to interview for this position. I will call you Monday afternoon to answer any questions you may have about my interests and experience.

Sincerely,

Darrell Baird

## Management Consultant

125 Jordan Street
New York, NY 10027

September 21, 19___

Donald West
MANAGEMENT INTERNATIONAL, INC.
742 West 29th Street
New York, NY 10013

Dear Mr. West:

Your ad in this week's issue of the <u>National Business Employment Weekly</u> for a Management Consultant coincides nicely with my interests and experience. I am very interested in this position and thus am submitting my resume for your consideration.

The ad states you are seeking an experienced manufacturing professional to assist in project work in North America and Europe. I would bring to this position the following relevant experience:

- 10 years operations management experience with competence in World-Class Manufacturing Systems (Total Quality Methods and Team-Based Employee Work Systems)

- 5 years management consulting work in six Western European and three Eastern European countries—fluent in German

In addition, I have been frequently cited by clients for my exceptional planning, communication, and interpersonal skills as well as demonstrated poise, discipline, and maturity.

My salary requirements are in the $60-$73K range, depending on the nature of responsibilities assigned to this position.

I will call you next Thursday afternoon to answer any questions you may have concerning my candidacy.

Sincerely,

Martin Goodman

# Word Processor

134 Marlow Street
Cincinnati, OH 45310

February 8, 19____

Sarah Anderson
Personnel Department
BENTON INTERNATIONAL
5541 Phillips Circle
Cincinnati, OH 45307

Dear Ms. Anderson:

I type 120wpm, I'm accurate, I'm proficient in WordPerfect 5.1, and I work well under pressure and with minimum supervision. Your ad in today's Cincinnati Star for a Word Processor states these as the desirable skills and qualities you hope to hire.

I have seven years of experience as a word processor. My last two employers also were contractors who faced numerous proposal deadlines that required dependable word processing capabilities. I've never missed a deadline and I willingly work overtime to get the job done.

I would appreciate an opportunity to interview for this position as well as demonstrate my word processing skills. I will call you on Friday to see if you wish to schedule such a meeting.

Sincerely,

Belinda Bower

## Manager/Retail Store

2761 Morrow Road
Rushing Falls, NY 10029

August 3, 19___

Janice Jackson
President
VILLAGE STORES
736 Main Street
Rushing Falls, NY 10026

Dear Ms. Jackson:

I read in today's <u>Post</u> of your opening for a manager with experience in women's retailing. I have 15 years experience in retailing of women's clothing—8 of those in management.

As my enclosed resume indicates, I have been acting manager of Chic Street for the past eight months. The manager of Chic Street will be returning next month following a leave of absence. I believe my management experience and retailing skills would be an asset at Village Stores.

Under my management at Chic Street we were able to:

- increase sales by 23%

- decrease employee turnover by 20%

- eliminate overtime

I am anxious to meet with you to discuss how we might be able to utilize my skills to increase the bottom line at the Village Store.

Sincerely,

Marilyn Chaffe

## Employment Counselor

766 Oro Rio Drive
San Luis Obispo, CA 98734

February 21, 19___

Bernard Tompkins, Manager
SUNSHINE TEMPORARY SERVICES
7638 Costa del Sur
Santa Barbara, CA 98763

Dear Mr. Tompkins:

For the past three years I have been an employment counselor with Solutions for Hire Temporary Services in San Luis Obispo. I like the opportunity to work with people—both the temporaries and the employers and enjoy helping them solve their employment problems.

I am responding to your advertisement for an employment counselor that appeared in today's edition of the Santa Barbara Sun Times. I will be moving to Santa Barbara in two weeks; I like my work so much that I would like to remain an employment counselor so your opening looks like a great opportunity.

I enclose my resume which will give you an overview of my background. Two of my accomplishments most pertinent to your advertised opening include:

- Started a new division in our office called "helping hands." This division, which provides unskilled workers to factories, has proven so successful our company has adopted the program in its branch offices nationwide.

- Initiated a temp-employer feedback program that has resulted in a 23% increase in business because of greater employer satisfaction with the temporary help we provide.

I look forward to meeting with you and having the opportunity to talk with you further regarding your needs and what I could bring to Sunshine Temporary Services.

Sincerely,

Jake Weber

# *Chapter Seven*

# COVER LETTERS
# WITH A DIFFERENCE

---

In contrast to Chapter Six, the cover letters appearing in this chapter fall into four major categories:

- referral cover letters
- telephone follow-up cover letters
- cold turkey cover letters
- broadcast cover letters

Each follows a different set of principles and probabilities for effectiveness. **Referral cover letters**, for example, are similar to several letters appearing in Chapter Five: they are written in response to a referral from a contact. These should be your most effective cover letters, because they are most likely written in the absence of competition, and because your "contact" has already screened you for the employer. Unlike referral letters—which are de- signed to get you information, advice, and referrals—these letters are aimed at getting a job interview.

**Telephone follow-up cover letters** are written in reference to job leads uncovered from telephone conversa- tions. If you use the telephone to de- velop job leads, you will undoubtedly write several of these cover letters. In most cases the "leads" you uncover through telemarketing will ask you to send a copy of your resume for their reference. While many of these re- quests are real and sincere and may lead to job interviews, others are polite ways of saying *"we are not interested but go ahead and send me something in writing if you wish."* Consequently, the effectiveness of these letters largely depends on the availability of real job vacancies.

**Cold turkey cover letters** are written without reference to a specific vacancy or the aid of a contact or referral. These are basically more personalized versions of the broadcast letter—they are addressed to a specific name. Don't expect many results from such letters, even with the help of the telephone follow-up. Employers hire in reference to specific vacancies—not in reference to nicely crafted resumes and letters. If they lack a vacancy, they will have little or no interest in your letter and resume. These letters merely play the probability game—sent out to hundreds of employers in the hope of uncovering a few vacancies which will soon arise or which were missed when surveying sources of job listings. While most of these letters are a waste of time and effort, occasionally you may receive a positive response as "luck comes your way."

**Broadcast cover letters** represent the ultimate "fishing expedition" for employers who may have job vacancies. Few if any of these letters ever result in a positive response. Some writers claim a two to five percent conversion rate—the percent of broadcast letters that turn into interviews. However, we have yet to see more than one percent of these letters going beyond the standard perfunctory reply:

> Thank you for your inquiry. While we do not have a vacancy available at present, we will keep your resume on file should our personnel needs change in the future.

Since the key to effectiveness is a real job vacancy coinciding with your qualifications, it may not make much difference what you say in these letters. The content of a broadcast cover letter may do little to enhance your resume or transform you into a serious applicant. Not surprising, sending a resume without a broadcast cover letter may be just as effective.

Our advice on broadcast cover letters and resumes is simple: use a strong opener to grab the reader's attention. Above all, you want the reader to remember you and your resume. This should be an exercise in good advertising copy, complete with an attention grabbing headline—the opening sentence and paragraph. Give it your best shot, but keep your expectations **very** low. Don't expect your telephone to begin ringing or your mailbox to fill up with positive responses. In the end, you probably have better things to do with your job search time. Concentrate, instead, on writing approach, thank you, and cover letters that respond to real job vacancies.

Similar to our examples in Chapter Six, the cover letters in this chapter, whenever possible, should end with a follow-up statement indicating what action you will take next. Again, the rule for making these letters effective is follow-up, follow-up, follow-up, follow-up.

# Referral Cover Letter

**THOMAS EVANS**

| 1901 Davis Road | Little Rock, AR 79831 | 719/319-4601 |
|---|---|---|

May 3, 19___

William Billings
Director of Training
MANAGEMENT TRAINERS INC.
319 Garner Street, Suite 130
Little Rock, AR 79831

Dear Mr. Billings:

Tracy Stevens recommended that I send you a copy of my resume. She said she spoke with you last week. You indicated that you might be looking for someone with a background in management training to work with two of your new clients.

I have nearly seven years of experience as both a training instructor and writer of management training materials. I have also written management training proposals which received funding through federal agencies. My instructional work has been with both government and corporate audiences ranging from entry-level to senior level executives.

I am prepared to teach a variety of one to five-day intensive courses on the following management subjects:

- Program Evaluation
- Supervision
- Supervising Former Colleagues
- Managing Organizational Change
- Problem Solving and Decision Making
- Benchmarking
- Time Management
- Managing Effective Meetings
- Conducting Management Control Reviews

I consistently receive "Excellent" to "Outstanding" evaluations from training participants. Since Tracy is familiar with my work, she can give you additional information on my background, experience, and skills.

I will call your office next Friday to answer any questions you may have about my work and to learn more about your future hiring needs.

Sincerely,


Thomas Evans

## Referral Cover Letter

2984 Independent Road
Wichita, KS 58722

April 19, 19___

Martha Williamson
MCR VIDEO PRODUCTIONS
8193 Center Street
Wichita, KS 58721

Dear Ms. Williamson:

Michael Thiel recommended that I send you a copy of my resume for your reference. He said he thought you might have an impending vacancy for a Computer Graphic Artist with experience in industrial video production. I have such a background.

I also enclose samples of my work. My background includes strong technical drawing and design skills. I regularly work with an Aurora 240 and MacIntosh. My formal training included work in animation.

Please let me know if you wish to see some of my other work. Since I've worked with Michael on previous video projects, he knows my work well. I'm sure he could answer any questions you may have about my qualifications.

I will call you on Tuesday to answer any questions you may have about my work. Perhaps we could get together to discuss your future graphic art needs.

Sincerely,

Grace Olson

# Referral Cover Letter

**BETTY HAUSER**

332 Westview Road          New Haven, CT 03813          291/382-2333

July 19, 19___

Michael Daniels, Editor
SCIENCE TODAY
1893 W. 27th St.
New York, NY 10013

Dear Mr. Daniels:

Gerald Reiter, your fraternity brother at UMC, recommended that I contact you about a possible position as a technical editor. He said you had mentioned the possibility of a vacancy arising in the very near future.

The enclosed resume summarizes my six years of experience as a technical writer. As the technical editor for a small scientific journal, I did all editing as well as some writing. Most recently I was in charge of supervising two assistant technical editors for a large scientific journal. I am especially good at translating scientific expressions into lay language.

I would appreciate being considered for the position of technical editor should it become vacant. I will call you next Thursday concerning my interest in the position.

Sincerely,

Betty Hauser

## Telephone Follow-Up Cover Letter

4381 Springfield Road
Charleston, WV 25841

December 3, 19____

Daryl James
ABLE TECHNOLOGY
813 Rockledge Drive
Charleston, WV 25841

Dear Mr. James:

Thanks so much for the taking the time to speak with me concerning your hiring needs. As you requested, I enclose my resume for your reference.

While you may not have an immediate need for a Computer Programmer, I would appreciate being kept in mind should your hiring needs change. As I mentioned over the phone, I have PL/1 and COBOL skills. In addition, I have over five years of experience with PRIME, FoxPro, UNIX, and X-Windows.

I'll check with you in a few weeks to see if your personnel situation has changed. I appreciate your consideration and look forward to meeting you at some later date.

Sincerely,

Steven Manley

# Telephone Follow-Up Cover Letter

**MARCIA ARMSTRONG**
227 South 7th Street
Joliet, IL 60993
319/713-0091

Shari Elkhart, Manager
FIRST ILLINOIS BANK
813 Tilden Parkway
Joliet, IL 60999

Dear Ms. Elkhart:

It was such a pleasure speaking with you today about your need for a Customer Service Representative. You indicated an impending vacancy as well as the possibility of creating another such position. As you requested, I'm enclosing a copy of my resume for your reference.

During the past three years I worked as a Customer Service Representative at Joliet Savings and Loan. There I was responsible for answering customer inquiries, opening new accounts, promoting new banking services, and handling customer complaints. I especially enjoyed working with new customers in familiarizing them with the institution's services.

I would appreciate being considered for one of your Customer Service Representative positions. I will call your office on Friday morning to answer any questions you may have about my interests and background.

Sincerely,

Marcia Armstrong

## Telephone Follow-Up Cover Letter

781 Lincoln Hwy.
Springfield, Il 62881

May 30, 19___

Peter Weston
ALLIED HEALTHCARE
913 West Finley Avenue
Springfield, IL 62876

Dear Mr. Weston:

I very much enjoyed talking with you today about your need for a Senior EDP Auditor. Our conversation got me thinking about both your needs and my future.

I had no idea John Clarkson had suggested me as a possible candidate for this position. While I remember speaking with John recently about my interest in working with a healthcare organization, I have not been actively pursuing a job change nor seriously contemplating a major move within the near future. However, your phone call got me thinking again about making such a career move.

I enclose a copy of my resume which you requested. I have over 10 years of increasingly responsible accounting experience. During the past five years I have been in charge of the EDP Audit function at Keegan Systems, Inc. I developed and expanded the company's programs, conducted audits of its management information system, and expanded computerized audits. I have experience in auditing large IBM system computers.

Your phone call was the catalyst for rethinking my future here at Keegan Systems, Inc. I would appreciate meeting with you soon to discuss how my interests and experience might best benefit Allied Healthcare. I'll call you this time—Wednesday afternoon—to see if you are still interested in pursuing my candidacy. In the meantime, I will have a chance to do some more thinking about what I would like to achieve at Allied Healthcare.

I look forward to meeting you soon.

Sincerely,

Patricia Dooley

## Cold Turkey Cover Letter

**SHELTON HULL**

159 Grand Avenue          Lincoln, NE 58271          713/820-6615

January 17, 19___

Julia Warner, Principal
LINCOLN HIGH SCHOOL
829 Main Street
Lincoln, NE 58270

Dear Ms. Warner:

Do you plan to hire Social Science teachers this coming year? If you do, I would appreciate being considered for a vacancy.

As indicated in the accompanying resume, I have a Master's degree in Political Science and five years of high school teaching experience. While my teaching experience has been with Department of Defense Schools in Europe, I do have a Nebraska teaching certificate which I acquired upon graduating from the University of Nebraska. I did my student teaching in Omaha, Nebraska.

After living abroad for five years, my wife and I plan to settle in the Lincoln area to pursue high school teaching careers. I believe my overseas teaching experience would be a real asset to Lincoln High School's social science program, especially given the momentous changes taking place today in Europe.

I will call you within the next 10 days to see if your hiring needs coincide with my training and experience. I appreciate your consideration.

Sincerely,

Shelton Hull

## Cold Turkey Cover Letter

198 Cherokee Trail
Marietta, GA 30932

October 3, 19____

Louis Paris
PARIS ADVERTISING
3901 Pickney Street
Marietta, GA 30930

Dear Mr. Paris:

Congratulations on receiving this year's Jaycee Award for outstanding business-person in Marietta. Succeeding in the advertising business indeed deserves recognition and applause. It's a tough business requiring tough and risky decisions. Above all, it requires talented people who know what they are doing. I know. I've been in the business for nearly 15 years.

When I read about your award in the Marietta Times, the article mentioned you were in the process of expanding your 22 employee firm to 30 employees. Would I be correct in assuming you will be looking for new talent?

I enclose a copy of my resume for your reference. I know the advertising business inside out. I've worked with both small and large firms and managed both small business and corporate accounts.

Could we meet at some mutually convenient time to discuss our mutual interests? I'll call your office next Thursday to see if your schedule would permit such a meeting.

Sincerely,

Charlene Parker

# Cold Turkey Cover Letter

**PORTER MACKEL**
3891 Terrace Lawn
Jacksonville, FL 35817
319/721-3827

October 3, 19\_\_\_

Martin Shephard
SOUTHERN REALTY
8189 King Street
Jacksonville, FL 35819

Dear Mr. Shephard:

Whoever said you can't get rich quick never met someone who made their fortune in real estate. While I may not be rich now, I will be soon. And I know I must first have to take some people with me. Those people will also be in real estate.

I've been a real estate agent for nearly four years. Last year I joined the $2 million club. Next year I plan to be in the $5 million club.

If you are looking for a top performer who knows how to sell and sell and sell, then we should talk soon. In the meantime, I enclose a copy of my resume for your reference.

I will call your office on Thursday afternoon to see if your schedule would permit us to meet in the very near future. Since I'm planning to move to another real estate firm within the next two months, I would really like to learn more about your firm and how I might fit into your plans for the future.

Sincerely,

Porter Mackel

# Broadcast Cover Letter

## GENE STALLINGS

291 Tremont Road                                          312/713-3921
Chicago, IL 60015

October 6, 19____

Would you like to see your sales increase by 30% within three months? You need not look further. I increased sales by 30% within three months of taking over and reorganizing our district sales force. I believe I can do the same for you.

The accompanying resume summarizes what I have done for others. If you are interested in what I can do for you, please call me at 312/713-3921.

Sincerely,

Gene Stallings

# Broadcast Cover Letter

**DAVID MARTIN**          7713 Montgomery Ave., St. Paul, MN 58219

717/389-9182

July 30, 19____

When was the last time you heard an employee say this— *"I'm not performing up to my ability but I promise you will see some major changes within the next three weeks."* I said this last year to my employer.

Three years ago I was so unhappy with my job that I nearly quit. I just didn't have the same level of enthusiasm and drive that I had in previous years. I thought maybe I should start a new career or just take off for a year to figure out what I really wanted to do with the rest of my life. Instead, I decided to rethink how I was doing my present job and perhaps reinvent my chosen career. Expecting to be fired, I went to my boss and told her I was unhappy with my performance. She was surprised at hearing such a confession since she considered me to be above average in comparison to other employees. I told her I could do much better than "above average" and I asked if I could take two weeks off to rethink what I really wanted to do. She agreed and I did my thinking.

It was the best two weeks I ever spent. I decided it was time to do things differently. I sat down and specified two goals I wanted to achieve over the next few years and five related goals to target over the new three months. Then I detailed how I would implement each goal and visualized the final outcomes in terms of percentage increases in productivity.

I returned to work with renewed enthusiasm and drive. Within two months I achieved my three month goals. I repeated this goal setting and visualizing exercise again and again until it is now automatically embedded into my daily routines.

I am no longer an "above average" employee. I am the top performer. My productivity has increased by more than 50%. I enjoy my work more than ever and look forward to each day with renewed energy.

If you are planning to expand your team to include more self-directed employees, please give me a call. I have more than 10 years of increasingly responsible experience in marketing. I believe I can do for you what I have done for previous employers—take charge and improve profitability. I'll tell you the truth about what I am doing, where I am going, and what I need to do to make my work better than ever.

Let's talk the next time you have a vacancy for someone with my goals and experience.

Sincerely,

David Martin

# Broadcast Cover Letter

## JANICE WHITE

8314 River Run              Pittsburgh, PA 17382              415/892-9831

June 7, 19__

What a great place to work!

That's what I and many others said only seven months ago—and then the sky fell. Who would have guessed that within three months Jamison Department Store would file Chapter 11 and then close its doors in another three months. A leveraged buyout engineered in New York City unfortunately killed what was one of Pittsburgh's finest department stores. Many former employers are still in shock.

I had six great years at Jamisons. I was responsible for the home furnishings department. We put on some wonderful special displays that nearly doubled our floor traffic during my last two years at Jamisons. In fact, my department was the second highest profit center for the Pittsburgh branch of Jamisons.

I am writing to you in the hope that you might have a current or forthcoming vacancy for someone with my interests, skills, and experience. If so, give me a call. I'm willing to relocate for the right challenge.

Sincerely,

Janice White

# Chapter Eight

# RESUME LETTERS

Resume letters are both a particular type of letter and a special type of resume. They are written in lieu of the cover letter/resume combination. A resume letter incorporates the experience sections of your resume in the format of an approach or application letter.

Resume letters have one major advantage over the more traditional letter-resume combination: they enable the writer to customize a resume and letter to respond to the specific needs of employers. This is especially important if the objective on your resume does not seem to fit the needs of the employer. A resume letter which includes a more precise employer-sensitive objective may serve you better than your generic resume.

Resume letters also have one major disadvantage: they don't look like resumes and thus may weaken your application. Individuals expecting to receive a cover letter and resume combination may view your resume letter as incomplete because it does not contain all the information they expect to receive in the traditional cover letter/resume combination.

Resume letters can be written for all types of job search situations. They can respond to vacancy announcements or function as cold turkey and broadcast letters, or as referral and telephone follow-up letters.

The examples in this chapter respond to different situations. Be sure to include a follow-up statement in your resume letter. Your phone call can make the difference between your resume just getting read versus being responded to in the form of a job interview and perhaps a job offer.

## Cold Turkey
(Research/Writing/Publications)

773 Main Street
Williamsburg, VA 23572

November 12, 19___

Barbara Thompson, President
SRM ASSOCIATES
421 91st Street
New York, NY 11910

Dear Ms. Thompson:

I just completed reading the article in <u>Business Today</u> on SRM Associates. Your innovative approach to recruiting minorities is of particular interest to me because of my background in public relations and minority recruitment.

I am interested in learning more about your work as well as the possibilities of joining your firm. My qualifications include:

- research and writing on minority recruitment and medical education
- secured funding and administered $845,000 minority representation program
- published several professional articles and reports on creative writing, education, and minorities
- organized and led public relations, press, and minority conferences
- M.A. in Journalism and B.A. in English

I will be in New York City during the week of December 10. Perhaps your schedule would permit us to meet briefly to discuss our mutual interests. I will call your office next week to see if such a meeting can be arranged.

I appreciate your consideration.

Sincerely yours,

Michele R. Folger

## Cold Turkey
(Trainer/Computers)

4921 Tyler Drive
Washington, DC 20011

March 15, 19___

Doris Stevens
STR CORPORATION
179 South Trail
Rockville, MD 21101

Dear Ms. Stevens:

STR Corporation is one of the most dynamic computer companies in the nation. Its model employee training and development program makes it the type of organization I am interested in joining.

I am seeking a training position with a computer firm which would use my administrative, communication, and planning abilities to develop effective training and counseling programs. My experience includes:

<u>Administration</u>:  Supervised instructors and counselors. Coordinated job vacancy and training information for businesses and schools.

<u>Communication</u>: Conducted over 100 workshops on interpersonal skills, stress management, and career planning. Frequent guest speaker to various agencies and private firms. Experienced writer of training manuals and public relations materials.

<u>Planning</u>: Planned and developed counseling programs for over 5,000 employees. Reorganized interviewing and screening processes and developed program of individualized and group counseling.

I am also completing my Ph.D. in industrial psychology with an emphasis on developing training and counseling programs for technical personnel.

Could we meet to discuss your program as well as how my experience might relate to your needs? I will call your office on Tuesday morning, March 23, to arrange a convenient time.

I especially want to show you a model employee counseling and career development program I recently developed. Perhaps you may find it useful for your work with STR.

Sincerely,

James C. Astor

## Vacancy Announcement
(Sales/Information Processing)

136 West Davis St.
Sacramento, CA 98771

September 5, 19___

Vicki Beatress
S.R. SYSTEMS
893 Mountain View Road
Sacramento, CA 98777

Dear Ms. Beatress:

I read with interest your ad in today's <u>Sacramento Star</u> for a Sales Associate. I'm especially interested in this position because of my previous experience in working with word processing equipment and corporate clients. I have been both a user and promoter of the systems you represent.

My experience and qualifications include seven years of progressive experience in the following positions:

- <u>Sales associate</u>: Represented both Savin and Ricoh word processers to corporate clients. Increased corporate accounts by 30% within 18 months. Recognized as the top Savin salesperson for the past three years. Linotech Systems, 1991 to present.

- <u>Office Manager</u>: Performed office management and materials production responsibilities. Planning and re-organized word processing center. Initiated time and cost studies which saved company $30,000 in additional labor costs. MCT Corporation (Vancouver, WA), 1986 to 1991.

I also recently completed my Bachelor's degree in business and computer science.

I believe my interests, skills, and experience are a good fit for this position. May I call you on Wednesday afternoon to answer any questions you may have concerning my candidacy?

Sincerely,

Wayne Watson

**Vacancy Announcement**
(Architectural Drafter)

1099 Seventh Avenue
Akron, OH 44522

February 1, 19____

Michael Abrams
THE LIGHTNER COMPANY
8113 Grand Avenue
Akron, OH 44520

Dear Mr. Abrams:

I am very interested in the Architectural Drafter position you advertised in today's <u>Akron Beacon</u>. This is exactly the type of position I have been seeking. It fits nicely with my technical knowledge and practical experience for enhancing construction design and building operations.

I would bring to this position nearly 10 years of progressively responsible experience in all phases of construction design:

<u>Draftsman</u>: Akron Construction Company, Akron. Helped develop construction plans for $14 million of residential and commercial construction. (1989 to present)

<u>Drafting Assistant/Apprentice</u>: R.T. Design Company, Akron. Served as an apprentice in helping design residential developments. Worked on the $130 million Lakeview Estate Development Center. (1985-1988)

<u>Cabinet maker</u>: Jason's Linoleum and Carpet Company, Akron. Designed and constructed kitchen counter tops and cabinets; installed the material in homes; cut and laid linoleum flooring in apartment complexes. (1983 to 1984)

<u>Carpenter's Assistant</u>: Kennison Associates, Akron. Assisted carpenter in the reconstruction of a restaurant and in building of forms for pouring concrete. (Summer 1982)

My training background includes completion of 15 hours of drafting courses at the Akron Vocational and Training Center.

I appreciate your consideration. I will call you on Monday afternoon to answer any questions you may have about my candidacy.

Sincerely,

John Albert

## Referral
(Public Relations/Conference Coordinator)

1234 Main Street
Norfolk, VA 23508

April 30, 19___

Dale Roberts
Business Manager
VIRGINIA BEACH CONVENTION CENTER
2981 Ocean Boulevard
Virginia Beach, VA 23519

Dear Mr. Roberts:

A mutual acquaintance of ours, Paul Amos, suggested that I contact you
about the new Virginia Beach Convention Center. He remarked that you are
developing a comprehensive public relations and marketing plan to attract
convention business.

As an officer of my local chapter and regional division of Toastmasters
International, I have acquired a substantial amount of public relations, special
events planning, and program coordination experience. Along with my professional work, my background includes working with diverse audiences, developing publicity campaigns and promotional materials, marketing services and
benefits, recruiting new members, handling financial records, and meeting
important deadlines. Furthermore, I have experience in writing and giving
speeches, chairing work groups, representing organizations, creative writing,
and teaching.

Since I have a strong interest in public relations-type activities and have a
thorough knowledge of our region and its resources, I was quite interested to
hear that your new marketing plan may use conference coordinators to work
with your sales staff. I would be very interested in learning more about your
plans and exploring future possibilities.

I plan to be near your office next week and wonder if we could have a brief
meeting? I'll give your office a call in the next few days to see if a mutually
convenient time could be arranged.

Sincerely,

Karen Jones

## Vacancy Announcement
(Management Information Systems)

2238 South Olby Road
Sacramento, CA 97342
May 22, 19___

Dorothy Avery
C.R. MANAGEMENT SYSTEMS
3817 Jefferson Street
Peoria, IL 61433

Dear Ms. Avery:

Your ad in today's <u>Peoria Journal Star</u> for a Management Information System Specialist caught my interest because it is ideally suited to my background.

I believe my past 15 years of work with the U.S. Navy in Systems Analysis and Management Information Systems has prepared me well for this position:

<u>Engineering Technician</u>: Reviewed technical publications to improve operational and technical descriptions and maintenance procedures. Developed system operation training course for high-level, nontechnical managers. Developed PERT charts for scheduling 18-month overhauls. Implemented a planning maintenance program and schedule for computer complex to reduce equipment down-time and increase utilization by user departments. (1988 to present)

<u>Assistant Manager/System Technicians</u>: Established and coordinated preventive/corrective maintenance system for four missile guidance systems resulting in increased reliability. Advised management on system operation and utilization for maximum effectiveness. Performed system test analysis and directed corrective maintenance actions. Interfaced with other managers to coordinate interaction of equipment and personnel. Conducted maintenance and safety inspections of various types of work centers. (1985 to 1987).

<u>Assistant Manager/System Technician</u>: Supervised system tests, analyzed results, and directed maintenance actions on two missile guidance systems. Overhauled and adjusted within factory specifications two special purpose computers, reducing down-time over 50%. Established and coordinated system and computer training program. Received the "Battle Efficiency E For Excellence" award in competition with others units. (1982 to 1984)

I would appreciate an opportunity to speak with you about how my experience can best meet your needs. I will call you on Wednesday to answer any questions.

Sincerely,

Gary Platt

## Referral
(Criminal Justice)

**CHERYL AYERS**

2589 Jason Drive                Ithaca, NY 14850                208/467-8735

April 20, 19___

Robert Byers
LAW ENFORCEMENT INSTITUTE
9881 Erie Road, Suite 203
Buffalo, NY 15283

Dear Mr. Byers:

Maryann Wilkerson, who interned with your department last year, suggested that I write to you concerning my interest in a research, data analysis, and planning position in law enforcement administration. She said you were planning to convert one of your internship positions to an entry-level position for a recent college graduate.

I will be graduating from Ithaca College in June with a B.S. in Criminal Justice. I majored in Law Enforcement Administration and minored in Management Information Systems. My G.P.A. is 3.6/4.0.

While my professional work experience is limited, I would bring to your organization the following demonstrated skills:

<u>Leadership</u>: Head secretary while working at State Police (past two years). Served as Rush Chair and Social Chair for Chi Phi Sorority. Elected Captain and Co-Captain three times during 10 years of cheerleading.

<u>Responsibility</u>: Handled highly confidential information, material, and files for State Police. Aided in the implementation of on-line banking system. In charge of receiving and dispersing cash funds for drive-in restaurant.

<u>Organization</u>: Revised ticket system for investigators' reports at State Police. Planned schedules and budget, developed party themes and skits, obtained prop material, and coordinated work of others during sorority rush.

<u>Data Analysis</u>: Program in Fortran, Cobal, and RPG II. Analyzed State Police data on apprehensions and wrote final report.

I would appreciate an opportunity to interview for this position. I will call you on Wednesday afternoon to answer any questions you may have concerning my candidacy.

Sincerely,

Cheryl Ayers

## Telephone Follow-Up
(Research)

**MICHELE R. FOLGER**
733 Main Street
Williamsburg, VA 23572
803/376-9932

September 27, 19___

Eric Johnson
THE POLICY INSTITUTE
1873 M Street, NW
Washington, DC 20037

Dear Mr. Johnson:

Thanks so much for taking the time to talk with me today about my interest in a research position with your organization. I learned a great deal about the Institute's work.

As I mentioned over the phone, I have over six years of research and program development experience with urban policy issues. This includes

Program Development: Conducted research on the representation of minority students in medical colleges. Developed proposal for a major study in the field. Secured funding for $845,000 project. Coordinated and administered the program which had major effect on medical education in the New York project area. Initiated and developed a national minority student recruitment program for 20 medical colleges.

Writing: Compiled and published reports in a variety of education areas. Produced several booklets on urban problems for general distribution. Published more than 20 articles in professional journals. Wrote and presented numerous conference papers.

Research: Gathered and analyzed information concerning higher education in a variety of specialized fields. Familiar with the latest data collection and statistical methods. Good knowledge of computers.

I enclose a sample of my work ("Representation of Minority Medical Students") for your reference. The article will appear in the October issue of Medical Educator.

I will call you next week to answer any questions you may have about my interests, skills, and experience.

Sincerely,

Michele Folger

# Broadcast
(Publishing/Computers)

**MARY FURNISS**
7812 W. 24th St.                                                                                    821/879-1124
Dallas, TX 71234

September 11, 19___

Do you ever wonder why some publishers accomplish the same production tasks for $500,000 less than others?

Three years ago I found an answer to this question which has now saved my employer more than $1 million. I may be able to do the same for you in this and other computer-related areas.

With over 10 years of experience in the publishing industry, I am now looking for a challenging opportunity that would build upon my previous experience:

Computer Applications Manager:  Managed all computer-related projects for publishing firm with annual sales of $40 million. Presented yearly capital expenditure and general systems budget, negotiated computer service contracts, evaluated and recommended new equipment and software purchases, and trained staff to use software and hardware. Replaced ATEX typesetting with desktop publishing system that immediately saved the company $650,000 in operational costs. Stevens Publishing Company, Fort Worth, TX, 1989 to present.

Editorial/Production Supervisor: Supervised all computer-related projects. Trained staff of 27 to use WordPerfect and other software applications. Devised an innovative system that transformed traditional galley editing into an efficient electronic editing system. New computerized system eliminated the need for two additional employees to handle the traditional galley editing system. Reduced errors by 70 percent. Benton Publishing Company, San Francisco, CA, 1986-1988

Editorial Assistant: Prepared annual Encyclopedia of International Forestry materials for editing and production. Supervised freelancers for special editorial projects. Proofread and copy-edited materials for 18 books produced annually. Received "Employee of the Year" award for initiating a new computerized editing system that saved the company $70,000 in annual freelance editing fees. Benton Publishing Company, San Francisco, CA, 1984-1985

If my skills fit your needs, I would love to talk to you about the possibility of joining your team on either a part-time or full-time basis. Please give me a call.

Sincerely,

Mary Furniss

### Vacancy Announcement
(Construction/Project Manager)

7781 West Gate Road
Cincinnati, OH 44411
March 22, 19___

Martin Drew
CONNERS CONSTRUCTION CO.
6661 Rowling Rock Rd.
Cincinnati, OH 44410

Dear Mr. Drew:

My skills and experience perfectly coincide with your announcement in today's
Cincinnati Observer for a Project Manager. I am seeking a challenging project
management position that would use my demonstrated skills to complete projects in
a timely and cost-effective manner.

I would bring to this position 28 years of progressively responsible construction
management experience involving all facets of construction, from start-up to final
inspection. I am experienced in supervising all aspects of construction including
masonry, concrete work, carpentry, electrical, mechanical, and plumbing. In addition, I communicate and work well with individuals at all levels, from clients to a
diverse mix of architects and subcontractors.

Highlights of my career include

Independent Contractor, Barstow & Thomas: Owned and managed a
general contracting company doing $8 million in commercial construction
each year. Performed all estimating, established contacts with subcontractors, purchased specialty items and materials, and handled shop drawings.
Completed most jobs within 30 days of projected completion dates and
managed to keep costs 5 percent under estimates. Cincinnati, 1981 to
1992.

Job Superintendent, J.P. Snow: Supervised all work from start-up to final
inspection as well as established all time schedules from start to finish.
Handled shop drawings, lab testing, job testing, change orders, daily reports, job progress reports, payroll, and hiring. Initiated an innovative
scheduling system that saved the employer more than $60,000 in projected
down-time. Consistently praised for taking initiative, providing exceptional
leadership, and communicating well with clients, architects, and subcontractors. Columbus, 1971-1980

I would appreciate an opportunity to interview for this position. I will call you
Tuesday afternoon to answer any questions you may have about my candidacy.

Sincerely,

James Barstow

## Referral
(Accountant)

443 West Capitol Street
Houston, TX 78261

March 4, 19___

Judith Holderman
SIMON AND TUCKER
8813 Tower Avenue, Suite 413
Houston, TX 78269

Dear Ms. Holderman:

While visiting my neighbor yesterday, I met Wendy Watson. After learning I was
in the process of making a job change, she suggested I contact you. She mentioned
you were recruiting for an Accounting/Finance position.

I have more than 10 years of increasingly responsible accounting and finance
experience:

Accountant:  Analyzed accounting systems and installed new IBM ledger
system for over 30 corporate accounts. Conducted training programs attended
by more than 500 accountants with small businesses. Developed proposals,
presented demonstration programs, and prepared reports for corporate clients.
Increased new accounts by 42% over a four year period. J.S. Conners & Co.,
Chicago, 1987 to present.

Junior Accountant: Acquired extensive experience in all aspects of corporate
accounting while assigned to the Controller's Office. Prepared detailed
financial records for corporate meetings as well as performed basic accounting tasks such as journal entries, reconciling discrepancies, and checking
records for accuracy and consistency. Assisted office in converting to a new
computerized accounting system that eliminated the need for additional
personnel and significantly improved the accuracy and responsiveness. Simon
Electrical Co., Chicago, 1983 to 1986.

Accounting Clerk: Acquired working knowledge of basic accounting functions
for a 200+ employee organization with annual revenues of $45 million.
Prepared journal vouchers, posted entries, and completed standard reports.
Proposed a backup accounting system that was implemented by the Senior
Accountant. Johnson Supplies, Chicago, 1980 to 1982.

Please let me know if you need any additional information. I will call you on
Thursday afternoon to answer any questions you may have about my interests,
skills, and experience.

Sincerely,


Mary Southern

## Telephone Follow-Up
(Paralegal)

771 Anderson Street
Knoxville, TN 38921

September 1, 19___

Mary Leonard
FORNAW, PETERS, AND LEWIS
3991 Jackson Blvd.
Knoxville, TN 38919

Dear Ms. Leonard:

Thank you for speaking with me today about opportunities in your firm for paralegals. Should a vacancy arise, I would appreciate being considered for a position in your firm. I would bring to your firm the following qualifications:

Law: Completed 36 semester hours of criminal justice course work with special emphasis on criminal law. Served as an intern with law firm specializing in criminal law. Interviewed clients, drafted documents, conducted legal research, assisted lawyers in preparing court briefs. Participated in criminal justice forums sponsored by the Department of Criminal Justice at the University of Illinois.

Research: Conducted research on several criminal cases as both a student and a paralegal intern. Experienced in examining court cases, interviewing lawyers and judges, and observing court proceedings. Proficient in using microfiche and computerized data bases for conducting legal research.

Communication: Prepared research papers, legal summaries, and memos and briefed attorneys on criminal cases relevant to assignments. Used telephone extensively for interviewing clients and conducting legal research.

Please let me know if you need any additional information. I will periodically check with you concerning impending vacancies.

Sincerely,

Charles Davis

# Vacancy Announcement
(Bookkeeper)

997 Mountain Road
Denver, CO 80222

June 4, 19___

James Fountain
SIMON WALTERS, INC.
771 George Washington Blvd.
Denver, CO 80220

Dear Mr. Fountain:

I read with interest your ad in today's <u>Rocky Mountain Times</u> for a bookkeeper. I believe my experience may be ideally suited for this position:

<u>Manager, Accounts Payable, T.L. Dutton, Denver</u>: Supervised 18 employees who routinely processed 200 invoices a day. Handled vendor inquiries and adjustments. Conducted quarterly accruals and reconciliations. Screened candidates and conducted annual performance evaluations. Reduced the number of billing errors by 30 percent and vendor inquiries by 25% within the first year. 1987 to present.

<u>Supervisor, Accounts Payable, AAA Pest Control, Denver</u>: Supervised 10 employees who processed nearly 140 invoices a day. Audited vendor invoices, authorized payments, and balanced daily disbursements. Introduced automated accounts receivable system for improving the efficiency and accuracy of receivables. 1984 to 1986.

<u>Bookkeeper, Davis Nursery, Ft. Collins</u>: Processed accounts payable and receivable, reconciled accounts, balanced daily disbursements, and managed payroll for a 20-employee organization with annual revenues of $1.8 million. 1981 to 1983.

<u>Bookkeeper, Jamison's Lumber, Ft Collins</u>: Assisted accountant in processing accounts payable and receivable and managing payroll for a 40-employee organization with annual revenues of $3.2 million.

I am currently taking advanced courses in accounting, computer science, and management at Colorado Junior College in Denver.

I will call you on Thursday afternoon to answer any questions you may have concerning my candidacy.

Sincerely,

Jane Barrows

## Cold Turkey
(Computers/Word Processing Sales)

136 W. Davis St.
Washington, DC 20030

January 7, 19___

James C. Thomas, President
ADVANCED TECHNOLOGY CORPORATION
721 West Stevens Road
Bethesda, MD 20110

Dear Mr. Thomas:

Advanced Technology's word processing equipment is the finest on the market today. I know because I have used different systems over the past eight years. Your company is the type of organization I would like to be associated with.

Over the next few months I will be seeking a sales position with an information processing company. My technical, sales, and administrative experience include:

Technical:  eight years operating Mag card and high speed printers: IBM 6240, MAG A,I,II,IBM 6640, and Savin word processor.

Sales:  recruited clients; maintained inventory; received and filled orders; improved business-community relations.

Administrative:  planned and re-organized word processing center; created new tracking and filing systems; initiated time and cost studies which reduced labor costs by $30,000 and improved efficiency of operations.

In addition, I have a bachelor's degree in communication with an emphasis on public speaking, interpersonal communication, and psychology.

Your company interests me very much. I would appreciate an opportunity to meet with you to discuss how my qualifications can best meet your needs. I will call your office next Monday, January 18, to arrange a meeting with you at a convenient time.

Sincerely yours,

Gail S. Topper

## Broadcast
(Financial Analyst)

**SUSAN ALLEN**

325 West End Street              Atlanta, GA 30019                402/378-9771

January 2, 19___

Are you looking for an investment analyst who will increase client investments by 20% each year? If so, let's talk about how I can do for you what I have done for previous employers.

With more than 10 years experience, I have a solid track record of performance. I would bring to your firm the following experience:

Investment Analyst, First City Bank, Atlanta:  Managed $650 million in diverse portfolios for bank's major clients which averaged 12 percent annual return on investment. Regularly met with clients, reviewed current investments, and presented new investment options for further diversifying portfolios. Introduced biweekly newsletter for communicating investment strategies with clients and bank officers. 1988 to 1991.

Research Analyst, Georgia Bank, Atlanta:  Conducted research, wrote reports, and briefed supervisor on stock market trends and individual companies which affected the bank's $1.2 billion securities portfolio. Worked closely with Investment Analyst in developing new approaches to communicating research findings and summary reports to clients and bank officers. 1985 to 1987

Research Assistant/Intern, Columbia Savings Bank, Columbia, SC: Served as a Summer Intern while completing undergraduate degree. Assigned as Research Assistant to Chief Analyst. Followed stock market trends and conducted research on selected investment banks. 1982.

I also have an MBA from the University of Miami. Concentrating on finance and management, my thesis was entitled Successful Investment Strategies of Florida's Ten Major Banks.

Please give me a call if your hiring needs coincide with my interests, skills, and experience.

Sincerely,

Susan Allen

## Vacancy Announcement
(Sales Manager)

7723 Stevens Avenue
Phoenix, AZ 80023

August 23, 19____

Cindy Morrow
HINES DEPARTMENT STORE
1831 Desert Blvd.
Phoenix, AZ 80021

Dear Ms. Morrow:

I am responding to your ad in today's <u>Phoenix Sun</u> for a Sales Manager. I would bring to this position twelve years of progressively responsible experience in all phases of retail sales and marketing with major discount stores. I annually improved profitability by 15 percent and consistently rated in the top 10 percent of the workforce. My experience includes

<u>Sales Manager, K-Mart, Memphis, TN</u>:  Managed four departments with annual sales of nearly $8 million. Hired, trained, and supervised a culturally diverse workforce of 14 full-time and 6 part-time employees. Reorganized displays, developed new marketing approaches, coordinated customer feedback with buyers in upgrading quality of merchandise, and improved customer service that resulted in 25 percent increase in annual sales. Received "Outstanding" performance evaluation and "Employee of the Year" award. 1987 to present.

<u>Assistant Buyer, Wal-Mart, Memphis, TN</u>:  Maintained inventory levels for three departments with annual sales of $5 million. Developed more competitive system of vendor relations that reduced product costs by 5 percent. Incorporated latest product and merchandizing trends into purchasing decisions. Worked closely with department managers in maintaining adequate inventory levels for best-selling items. 1983 to 1986.

<u>Salesperson, Zayres, Knoxville, TN</u>:  Responsible for improving sales in four departments with annual sales of $3.5 million. Reorganized displays and instituted new "Ask An Expert" system for improved customer relations. Sales initiatives resulted in a 20 percent increase in annual sales. Cited for "Excellent customer relations" in annual performance evaluation. Worked part-time while completing education. 1980-1982.

Please consider this letter to be my application for this position. I will call you next Friday morning to answer any questions you may have about my candidacy.

Sincerely,

Mark Able

## Referral
(Military/Attorney)

**STEVEN MARSH**

2001 West James Ct. ▪ Seattle, WA 98322 ▪ 501/789-4321

October 31, 19___

Morton Gates
BOEING CO.
1141 Washington Avenue
Seattle, WA 98181

Dear Mr. Gates:

John Miles recommended that I contact you about my interest in aviation law. Since I will be retiring from the U.S. Air Force next May, I am exploring career opportunities with companies interested in my expertise in aviation law. John said you were in the process of creating a new position dealing with structured settlements, an area in which I have had major responsibility when working at Headquarters in Washington, DC.

My legal experience with the Air Force includes the following duties, responsibilities, and accomplishments:

<u>Chief Circuit Defense Counsel, Davis Air Force Base, Ogden, UT</u>: Personally defended all Flying Evaluation Boards (4), winning every one. Successfully defended felony trials covering offenses of drug use, distribution, assault, DUI, and perjury. Supervised, trained, and directed 22 attorneys and 17 paralegals responsible for total defense services across 16 Air Force installations located in 12 states. Included oversight of over 500 trials with every offense up to and including premeditated murder. 1988-present

<u>Chief, Aviation Settlement Branch, U.S. Air Force, Washington, DC</u>: Directed the investigation, adjudication, and either settlement or litigation of all aviation, environmental, medical malpractice, and other tort claims filed against the Air Force. In 1988, this topped a $40 billion dollar exposure with the percentage of payout to claimed amount the lowest in over a decade. Supervised staff of 13 attorneys and 5 paralegals. Reformulated U.S. Air Force policy on tort claim and litigation matters in conjunction with the Department of Justice leading to a better concept and application of paying the losers and spending time and resources to win-the-winners. 1986-1987

<u>Chief, Tort Section, U.S. Air Force, Washington, DC</u>: Supervised the investigation and recommended adjudication or litigation of all aviation tort claims against the Air Force, including the last of the Agent Orange cases and the KAL 007 Korean airliner shoot-down by the Soviet Union. Supervised staff of 3 attorneys and 1 paralegal. Recommended U.S. Air Force policy change on aviation tort claims that directly resulted in greater Agency latitude for meritorious claims independent of the previously required GAO Office requirements. 1985

<u>Staff Judge Advocate, Stevens Air Force Base, Miami, FL</u>: Advised top management of all legal issues to include the convening of Aircraft Accident Boards and Flying Evaluation Boards. Directed tort, labor, environmental, procurement, and criminal law procedures. During this period, defended two state environmental Notice of Violations successfully, and over 40 criminal cases were prosecuted without a single acquittal. Served as management's Chief Labor Resolution Negotiator securing settlements at 60 percent of the previously approved maximums. Supervised staff of 4 attorneys and 5 paralegals. 1982-1984

<u>Assistant Staff Judge Advocate, Lowry Air Force Base, CO</u>: Served as government prosecutor for over 35 trials with no acquittals. Served as government representative in over 20 administrative hearings with no losses. Counseled clients on rights/duties under state and federal law. 1978-1981

<u>Area Defense Counsel, Marshall Air Force Base, Austin, TX</u>: Defended over 300 clients in criminal trials, administrative hearings, or minor disciplinary concerns. 1977

Please let me know if you need any additional information. I will call you next week concerning my interest in Boeing. I look forward to speaking with you.

Sincerely,

Steven Marsh

## Broadcast
(International/Construction)

1131 N. Bridge Road
Baltimore, MD 21027

December 7, 19___

I am interested in an overseas construction management/supervision position with an international design/build firm. My experience includes

Management:  Owner and President for 14 years of a design/build firm with annual revenues between $1 and $2 million

Construction:  Direct experience with most methodologies of construction including wood frame, masonry, and light metal.

Supervision:  Responsible for 15 full-time employees. Concurrently supervised several hundred sub-contractors/crews. Many crews were non-English speaking.

Architectural design:  Residential experience with custom and track family homes ranging from 1,000 to 10,000 square feet. Commercial experience with retail, office, office/warehouse, warehouse, restaurants, and marinas.

Overseas:  Fluent in German, written and spoken. Experienced working, researching, and residing abroad—11 years in northern Europe and several Third Word countries.

If my interests, skills, and experience coincide with your hiring needs, I would appreciate hearing from you. I can be contacted at 301/111-0981.

Sincerely,

George Willington

# Chapter Nine

# FOLLOW-UP LETTERS

Your letters and resumes are only as good as your follow-up methods. While the most efficient and effective follow-up method will be the telephone, on occasion you may want to write follow-up letters. This normally occurs when you cannot get the phone number of the letter recipient or the letter recipient does not return your phone call after repeated attempts to contact them. These follow-up letters are initiated by you in an attempt to get your letter recipient to take action related to the content of your letter.

At the same time, you may write several follow-up letters in response to information received from or requests made by others. For example, your follow-up telephone call may result in a request to send samples of your work or to complete an application or other type of form. These follow-up letters are extremely important because you now have a foot, however tentative, in someone's door.

Whatever you do, treat these follow-up letters with tender loving care! They may be your ticket to the next step—a job interview.

## PERSISTENCE PAYS OFF

Conducting a telephone follow-up is easier said than done. Many vacancy announcements purposefully avoid identifying their organization by name and telephone in order to avoid walk ins and telephone calls. Even when you have a name and telephone number, many employers prefer not taking phone calls from applicants simply because they are not prepared to talk with you about a hiring decision and don't want to be forced into making a decision by an assertive applicant. They would rather you went away and waited for them to contact you. You may call several times and be told by a gatekeeper that the individual is *"on the other line," "in a meeting," "not available at this time,"* or *"she will get back with you later."* In many cases these are code words for not wanting to speak with you. A gatekeeper takes your name, phone number, and message but you never receive a return call. After making three to five such unsuccessful follow-up calls, it's time to write a follow-up letter instead.

## WHEN TO WRITE

The follow-up letters in this chapter serve as alternatives to the follow-up telephone call. If you have not received a reply to your initial letter within two weeks, it's safe to assume you will not be receiving a reply at all. Begin making your follow-up telephone calls after one week to ten days. If the phone calls do not pay off within three days, go ahead and write a follow-up letter. Waiting any longer will probably be a waste of time.

## IMPORTANT ENCLOSURES

The most effective follow-up letters should include two items—a copy of your original letter and mention of your telephone number for convenience in responding to you. If you are requesting information, you may want to include a self-addressed stamped envelope for convenience of the letter recipient.

## CONTROL YOUR EMOTIONS

If you are angry after making six follow-up telephone calls and you still receive no response (what jerks!), try not to express your disappointment or feelings in your follow-up letter. Keep your tone positive and up beat. Persistence in a friendly and professional manner will eventually pay off with a response.

## Information Request

124 Linden Place
Chicago, IL 60002

October 15, 19___

Mindi Mason, Director
ENVIRONMENTAL RESEARCH CENTER
147 Gilbert Avenue
San Francisco, CA 91441

Dear Ms. Mason:

On October 2, I wrote to you requesting information on organizations involved in conducting environmental research on tropical rain forests. Since I have not heard from you, I assume you may not have received my original letter.

I enclose a copy of the original letter for your reference. I would appreciate whatever assistance you could give me. Should you need to call, I can be reached at 410/381-8214.

Sincerely,

Steven Wallace

## Placement Services

853 West Norton Road
Boise, ID 88344

July 22, 19___

James Walters, Director
Information Services
ASSOCIATION OF
    AMERICAN ACCOUNTANTS
5391 Tyler Road
Washington, DC 20543

Dear Mr. Walters:

Did you receive the enclosed letter? I wrote it on July 8, but did not have your name at that time. Perhaps it was forwarded to the wrong person.

As I mentioned in my earlier letter, I would appreciate information on your placement or job search services. If you don't have such information, can you recommend any other organizations that might provide such assistance to accountants?

Should you want to contact me by phone, my number is 818/371-9821. I appreciate your assistance.

Sincerely,

George Miles

## Alumni Network Information

973 West End
New York, NY 10001

March 10, 19____

Wanda Evans, Director
Alumni Services
UNIVERSITY OF
   SOUTHERN CALIFORNIA
1933 Jasper Street
Los Angeles, CA 90312

Dear Ms. Evans:

I am having difficulty getting information on the USC alumni group in
Houston. As indicated in the enclosed copy of my letter to you on February
13, I would like to make contacts with fellow alumni concerning my interests
in international investment banking.

Could you please let me know if you have such information? I tried calling
your office several times but was told you were not available. I enclose a
self-addressed stamped envelope for your convenience. My phone number is
317/892-9881.

I appreciate your assistance.

Sincerely,

Brenda Carpenter

## Placement Assistance

246 Cathedral Drive
Salt Lake City, UT 86732

July 15, 19____

James Martin
Association Referral Service
U.S. CHAMBER OF COMMERCE
1615 H St., NW
Washington, DC 20062

Dear Mr. Martin:

Did you get my letter of June 3? Assuming it got lost along with way, I enclose a copy of the original for your reference.

I am interested in receiving information on employment opportunities in Western Europe. For your convenience, I enclose a self-addressed stamped envelope. I also can be reached at 818/839-9193.

Many thanks for your assistance.

Sincerely,

Sandra Vertimosa

## Information on Company

4439 Center Street
Portland, OR 98211

February 20, 19___

Melaine Roberts, Director
Public Relations Office
TRC PHARMACEUTICAL COMPANY
1000 West Knight Street
Terre Haute, IN 48732

Dear Ms. Roberts:

Did you get my letter of January 30? I enclose a copy for reference as well as a self-addressed stamped envelope for your convenience.

As I mentioned in my earlier letter, I am conducting research on various pharmaceutical companies as part of a career development project. I would really appreciate information on TRC Pharmaceutical Company.

Thank you in advance for your assistance.

Sincerely,

Jeffrey Williams

## Relocation Services

9341 Capitol Street
Omaha, NE 54371

March 15, 19____

David Allison, Director
Relocation Department
CENTURY 21
9431 Sheridan Road
Austin, TX 77211

Dear Mr. Allison:

Thanks so much for your prompt reply to my letter of March 3 for information on housing in the Austin community. The maps, brochures, and other publications were most helpful in giving us a good overview of the Austin housing market.

Could you do us one more favor? Our handicapped daughter needs special education services. Which schools would provide such services and how close are they to the neighborhoods you identified in your letter of March 7?

We look forward to hearing from you and meeting with you when we visit Austin next month.

Sincerely,

Janice Wilson

## Subscription and Referral Services

113 Bellflower Ct.
Orono, ME 08013

August 23, 1992

April Burgess
Subscription Manager
ACCESS: Networking in the
    Public Interest
50 Beacon Street
Boston, MA 02108

Dear Ms. Burgess:

Thanks so much for your prompt response to my letter of August 9 for subscription and referral services. I enclose a check for $30 to cover the four-month subscription to Community Jobs.

I would also like to take advantage of your job matching services for an additional $20. Therefore, I enclose a copy of my resume, a completed data form, and check to initiate my participation in this data bank program.

I look forward to receiving my first issue of your publication.

Sincerely,

Stacey Chino

## Information and Employment Services

1134 Stanford Lane
Orlando, FL 31339

July 23, 19____

Janice Eaton
HIGH TEMPS
73 Weston Road
Suite 913
Orlando, FL 31341

Dear Ms. Eaton:

Thanks for sending me information on your temporary employment
services. I completed and am returning the registration and background
information form you sent me. I also enclose a copy of my resume which I
revised since sending you my resume on July 11. Please replace the one you
have on file with this "new improved" version.

I look forward to meeting you next Monday at 10:30am to discuss how my
interests and experience might best meet the needs of your clients.

Sincerely,

Martin Davis

## Assessing Job Search Services

5431 Atlanta Blvd.
Atlanta, GA 33479

May 9, 19___

Thomas Allen
HALDANE ASSOCIATES
848 Peachtree Plaza
Atlanta, GA 33481

Dear Mr. Allen:

Thank you for sending me information on your career counseling services. I have had a chance to review the sample contract you sent. I fully understand that you provide career counseling and job search services rather than job placement services. I believe this is exactly what I need at this stage of my job search.

Could we meet to further discuss my needs and how Haldane Associates would work with me over a two month period? I'm still not clear about the actual process I would be involved in. Perhaps you could answer a few questions some friends have raised about contracting for such services. I've been told I can do all of this work on my own without hiring a firm such as yours. I'm still not sure I'm doing the right thing. Perhaps you could enlighten me on why it would be in my best interests to sign a contract with Haldane Associates. I'm especially interested in learning what happened to others who have used your services.

Please let me know when we might be able to meet. My phone number is 717/293-1240.

Sincerely,

Paul Martinez

## Information

752 Thompson Court
Albany, NY 14321

March 23, 19___

James Reston
HEALTH SYSTEMS RECRUITERS, INC.
918 Monroe Street
Chicago, IL 60021

Dear Mr. Reston:

Thank you for your letter of April 2, in which you requested I complete
the enclosed Career Fact Sheet for your records. I appreciate your willingness
to include me in your recruitment circle.

In response to your question concerning my availability for overseas
assignments, my answer is both yes and no. Since I have worked abroad for
more than six years, I have no problem operating in the international arena.
Indeed, I have very much enjoyed my international work and look forward to
continuing it in the near future. However, my personal situation—single
mother—is such that I prefer short-term assignments rather than residence
abroad. My two children will enter high school during the next two years. I
believe it's important that they experience their high school years here in the
States. My ideal situation would be to travel abroad on assignments for no
more than six to eight weeks each year.

I look forward to working with you over the coming weeks. Please give
me a call if you have any questions: 204/381-0991.

Sincerely,

Doris Luffert

## Rejecting Employment Service

8801 West End St.
Cleveland, OH 45313

January 13, 19____

Rob Richards
JOBS ABROAD
203 Ocean Blvd.
Ft. Lauderdale, FL 31111

Dear Mr. Richards:

I appreciated your prompt reply to my inquiry of December 29 about jobs in Australia. However, I must decline your service. I understand you are asking me to send you a check for $165 so you can help me find a job in Australia.

I'll keep my $165. A friend told me they used a similar service that sent them a travel video and a 10-page listing of names and addresses he could have gotten by spending 10 minutes in the public library. In addition, I called the Better Business Bureau in Ft. Lauderdale and learned they never heard of you or your company. Therefore, I've decided not to take a chance on paying money for what could be another unpleasant experience reported by others who have used similar services.

Please do not share my name and address with other firms.

Sincerely,

Daryl Peterson

## Information Needs

### THOMAS EVANS

1901 Davis Road          Little Rock, AR 79831          719/319-4601

May 16, 19___

William Billings
Director of Training
MANAGEMENT TRAINERS INC.
319 Garner Street, Suite 130
Little Rock, AR 79831

Dear Mr. Billings:

Thank you for your letter of May 11 in response to my earlier inquiry concerning management training opportunities with MTI.

As you requested, I enclose copies of course outlines for the two most popular courses I teach:

- Program Evaluation
- Managing Effective Meetings

During the past three years I have instructed over 300 individuals in each of these courses. I also enclose a sampling of evaluation comments I've received from participants during the past six months.

As I mentioned earlier, I also have developed the course materials for each of these courses. Each trainee receives a 100+ page loose-leaf training manual as part of their course materials. The manual, which is designed to be self-directed, has become very popular with several organizations that now purchase it separately for employees who are unable to attend my three-day workshop. I think there is a good market here for additional training materials. Perhaps you would be interested in discussing how my work with training materials could potentially evolve into a profit center for MTI.

Please give me a call if you need any additional information. I look forward to meeting you soon to discuss our mutual interests.

Sincerely,


Thomas Evans

## Request For More Information

2984 Independent Road
Wichita, KS 58722

April 29, 19___

Martha Williamson
MCR VIDEO PRODUCTIONS
8193 Center Street
Wichita, KS 58721

Dear Ms. Williamson:

Thank you for speaking with me today about your graphic art needs. As you requested, I enclose a sample video of my animation work.

I believe this video adequately represents my graphic art interests and skills. Most of this work was completed on an Aurora 240.

As I mentioned in my letter of April 19, Michael Thiel should be able to answer other questions you may have about my work.

I look forward to meeting you soon.

Sincerely,

Grace Olson

## Confirming Appointment

781 Lincoln Highway
Springfield, IL 62881

June 22, 19___

Peter Weston
ALLIED HEALTHCARE
913 West Finley Avenue
Springfield, IL 62876

Dear Mr. Weston:

I enjoyed speaking with you today about your vacancy for a Senior EDP Auditor. Yes, I am still interested in this position.

I look forward to meeting you next Thursday at 1:30pm to discuss how my interests and experience can best meet your accounting needs. If you don't mind, I will bring a sample of my work with me. I'm especially interested in sharing with you some changes I've made in the EDP Audit function which seem to work well in reducing accounting costs.

Sincerely,

Patricia Dooley

# Job Inquiry

**SHELTON HULL**

159 Grand Avenue            Lincoln, NE 58271            713/820-6615

September 25, 19___

Julia Warner, Principal
LINCOLN HIGH SCHOOL
829 Main Street
Lincoln, NE 58270

Dear Ms. Warner:

Last January I wrote to you inquiring about possible vacancies for Social Science teachers. When I spoke to you over the phone, you indicated you were under a hiring freeze due to budgetary cuts affecting your staffing levels.

I enclose a copy of my newly revised resume for your reference. It reflects additional teaching experience and training I received during this past year.

Please keep me in mind should your hiring needs change. Hopefully we will be seeing fewer budgetary freezes for education this coming year!

Sincerely,

Shelton Hull

## Vacancy Announcement

136 West Davis St.
Sacramento, CA 98771

September 15, 19___

Vicki Beatress
S.R. SYSTEMS
893 Mountain View Road
Sacramento, CA 98777

Dear Ms. Beatress:

On September 5, I sent you a copy of the attached letter in application for a Sales Associate position. Have you had a chance to make any preliminary decisions?

I want to reiterate my interest in this position and availability for an interview. I believe my interests, skills, and experience are an excellent fit for this position.

I will call you next Thursday to answer any questions you may have about my candidacy.

Sincerely,

Wayne Watson

## Interview Confirmation

1234 Main Street
Norfolk, VA 23508

April 30, 19____

Dale Roberts
Business Manager
VIRGINIA BEACH CONVENTION CENTER
2981 Ocean Boulevard
Virginia Beach, VA 23519

Dear Mr. Roberts:

Just a quick note to reconfirm our appointment next Tuesday at 10:30am. I look forward to discussing with you how my interests, skills, and experience can promote the Virginia Beach Convention Center.

As you requested, I enclose a copy of my resume for your reference. Please let me know if you need any additional information before our meeting on Tuesday.

Sincerely,

Karen Jones

## Vacancy Announcement

**CHERYL AYERS**

2589 Jason Drive                    Ithaca, NY 14850                    208/467-8735

April 27, 19____

Robert Byers
LAW ENFORCEMENT INSTITUTE
9881 Erie Road, Suite 203
Buffalo, NY 15283

Dear Mr. Byers:

When I called your office today, I learned you would be out of town until next Thursday. I was calling in reference to my letter of April 20 in which I inquired about an impending research, data analysis, and planning position.

I will call you again next Friday to discuss my continuing interest in working with the Law Enforcement Institute.

Sincerely,

Cheryl Ayers

## Vacancy Announcement

997 Mountain Road
Denver, CO 80222

June 11, 19\_\_\_

James Fountain
SIMON WALTERS, INC.
771 George Washington Blvd.
Denver, CO 80220

Dear Mr. Fountain:

I'm not doing well in the telephone department. I called your office several times yesterday but was unable to get through to you. After my sixth try I decided Thursday was one of your incredibly busy days. And you really didn't need another phone call to top off your day!

I was just following up on my letter of June 4 in application for the book-keeper position you had advertised in last week's <u>Rocky Mountain Times</u>. Have you had a chance to review my application? I also wanted to let you know that I am still interested in this position and would appreciate an opportunity to meet with you to discuss how my interests, skills, and experience can best contribute to sound financial reporting at Simon Walters, Inc.

I'll try to call you again next Tuesday. Perhaps your schedule will be less hectic by that time.

Sincerely,

Jane Barrows

## Vacancy Announcement

**ROBBIN BARRETT**

221 Western Ave.                Detroit, MI 47892                919/231-3214

November 13, 19___

Katherine Kerry
Recruitment Director
CONSUMER UNION
29 Temple Place
Boston, MA 02111

Dear Ms. Kerry:

Thank you for speaking with me today concerning my application for the Consumer Program Associate position. Your description of the position better clarified my understanding of how this position fits into the larger operations of the Consumer Union.

I want to reiterate my continuing interest in this position. Indeed, after learning the position will involve creating new citizen outreach offices— something I've been very active and successful in doing for the past three years—I'm more interested than ever in working with the Consumer Union. This is the type of grassroots activity I most enjoy. It's also a good organizational strategy for building the networks necessary for mobilizing public support behind Consumer Union's environmental protection efforts.

Please let me know if you need any additional information about my candidacy. I look forward to meeting you in the very near future to discuss how I see this position evolving both within Consumer Union and at the community level.

Sincerely,

Robbin Barrett

## Vacancy Announcement

712 W. Vermont St.
Washington, DC 20132

May 9, 19____

Elliott Stevens
WASHINGTON MONTHLY
1611 Connecticut Ave., NW
Washington, DC 20009

Dear Mr. Stevens:

Just a quick note to clarify my continuing interest in the Summer Circulation Intern position I applied for on May 3. As I discussed with you over the phone today, I was not sure whether I wanted to intern on a part-time or full-time basis this summer. Please don't get me wrong. I don't mean to appear indecisive nor disinterested. I just didn't think about the possibility that this would be a full-time position. For some reason I was led to believe, based upon conversations with other classmates who have interned, that most Summer Internship positions were part-time. Now I know better.

After talking with you, I decided to set some priorities in relation to this position and my career interests. What I really want is a full-time position. I think I will both contribute and learn the most by interning on a full-time basis during the next three months.

Will you be scheduling interviews for this position soon? I would appreciate the opportunity to further discuss how my interests and skills could be best used in this position.

Sincerely,

Tracey Nelson

**Vacancy Announcement**

2908 Trail Drive
Atlanta, GA 32119

October 9, 19____

Barbara Haynes
Department of Dispute Resolution
SUPREME COURT OF GEORGIA
100 N. Eight Street, 2nd Floor
Atlanta, GA 32109

Dear Ms. Haynes:

Thanks so much for taking time from your busy schedule to discuss my
application for the position of Dispute Resolution Intake Coordinator in DeKalb
County.

I agree with you that this position should involve a major grantsmanship
component. New federal monies are now available through the Department of
Justice to fund experimental dispute resolution programs. I'm also aware of a
little known grant program in the Department of Housing and Urban Development for mediating jurisdictional disputes within urban counties. And I believe a
new Cooperative Agreement program dealing with mediation programs will be
announced through the Department of Justice within the next six months. The
new Dispute Resolution Intake Coordinator should explore these and other
programs for DeKalb County.

I appreciated your time in discussing this position and your program. As I
indicated in my letter of September 29, I have a strong interest in this position
and working with your organization. This is one of the most innovative programs I have encountered anywhere in the country. It deserves a Dispute
Resolution Intake Coordinator who has the necessary entrepreneurial skills to
sustain and expand a successful program.

I would appreciate an opportunity to meet with about this position. I have
several other ideas I would like to share with you on grantsmanship skills
appropriate for the position. Should you have any questions, my number is
313/781-9831.

Sincerely,

Kevin Anderson

## Vacancy Announcement

**WANDA PETERS, RN**
213 Padra Fara, Apt. 137
Manila, The Philippines

June 27, 19___

Doris Silverman, MS, RN
Nurse Recruiter
OREGON GENERAL REHAB CENTER
8187 Elkins Drive
Portland, OR 98309

Dear Ms. Silverman:

As a follow-up to my June 23 letter of application for the Rehab Nurse position, I wanted to let you know that my schedule for returning to the States is now final. I will arrive in Portland on July 17. Assuming the position may still be vacant, could we meet sometime during the week of July 19 to discuss my candidacy?

I will call your office as soon as I arrive in Portland to see if your schedule would permit such a meeting.

Sincerely,

Wanda Peters, RN

## Vacancy Announcement

717 Georgia Avenue
Indianapolis, IN 48712

March 9, 19____

Barry Bates
Human Resources
GREATER INDIANAPOLIS HOSPITAL
67100 Conners Road
Indianapolis, IN 48712

Dear Mr. Bates:

Thanks so much for returning my call today. I appreciated your thoughtfulness and learned a great deal about your needs and the nature of the Occupational Therapist position.

As you requested, I instructed my university placement office to send you a copy of my file. It includes transcripts, three letters of recommendation, and a sample of my work. Since I requested these documents be sent to you by Federal Express, they should reach you within two days.

I'll give you a call next week to answer any additional questions you may have about my interest in this position.

Sincerely,

Susan Wright

# Chapter Ten

# THANK YOU LETTERS

Thank you letters are some of the most powerful job search letters you will ever write. If you are like many other job seekers, your thank you letters will be more effective than your resume and cover letters. One well written and timed thank you letter may become the key to being invited to an interview or offered the job.

## GET REMEMBERED AS THOUGHTFUL

Why are short and simple thank you letters so effective in a job search—especially when compared to lengthier and more substantive job search letters and resumes?

Thank you letters demonstrate an important **social grace** that says something about you as an individual—your personality and how you probably relate to others. They communicate an important characteristic sought by many employers—**thoughtfulness**.

Better still, since few individuals write thank you letters, those who do write them are **remembered** by letter recipients. And one thing you definitely want to happen again and again during your job search is to be remembered by individuals who can provide you with useful information, advice, and referrals as well as invite you to job interviews and extend to you job offers. For being remembered as a thoughtful person with the proper social graces will give you an edge over many other job seekers who fail to write thank you letters. Whatever you do, make sure you regularly send thank you letters in response to individuals who assist you in your job search.

> *Being remembered as a thoughtful person with the proper social graces will give you an edge over many other job seekers.*

Many job seekers discover the most important letters they ever wrote were thank you letters. These letters can have several positive outcomes:

- **Contacts turn into more contacts and job interviews:** A job seeker sends a thank you letter to someone who recommended they contact a former college roommate; impressed with the thoughtfulness of the job seeker and feeling somewhat responsible for helping her make the right contacts, the individual continues providing additional referrals, which eventually lead to two job interviews.

- **Job interview turns into a job offer:** A job seeker completes a job interview. Within 24-hours he writes a nice thank you in which he expresses his gratitude for having an opportunity to interview for the position as well as reiterates his interest in working for the employer. This individual is subsequently offered the job. The employer later tells him it was his thoughtful thank you letter that gave him the edge over two other equally qualified candidates who never bothered to follow-up the interview.

- **A job rejection later turns into a job offer:** After interviewing for a position, a job seeker receives a standard rejection letter from an employer indicating the job was offered to another individual. Rather than get angry and end communications with the employer, the job seeker sends a nice thank you letter in which she notes her disappointment in not being selected and then thanks him for the opportunity to interview for the position. She also reiterates her continuing interest in working for the organization. The employer remembers this individual. Rather than let her get away, he decides to create a new position for her.

- **A job offer turns into an immediate positive relationship:** Upon receiving a job offer, the new employee sends a nice thank you letter in which he expresses his appreciation for the confidence expressed by the employer. He also reassures the employer that he will be as productive as expected. This letter is well received by the employer who is looking forward to working closely with such a thoughtful new employee. Indeed, he becomes a mentor and sponsor who immediately gives the employee some plum assignments that help him fast-track his career within the organization.

■ **Termination results in strong recommendations and a future job offer:** An employee, seeking to advance her career with a larger organization, receives a job offer from a competing firm. In submitting her formal letter of resignation, she also sends a personal thank you letter to her former employer. She sincerely expresses her gratitude for having the opportunity to work with him and attributes much of her success to his mentoring. This letter further confirms his conclusion about this former employee—he's losing a valuable asset. While he cannot offer her a similar or better career opportunity in this organization, he will keep her in mind if things change. And things do change two years later when he makes a major career move to a much larger organization. One of the first things he does as Vice-President is to begin shaping his own personal staff. He immediately

contacts her to see if she would be interested in working with him. She's interested and soon joins her former employer in making another major career move.

In these cases it was the job seekers' thank-you letters, rather than their cover letters and resumes, that gave them the edge and landed them job interviews and offers.

As indicated in the above scenarios, thank you letters should be written in the following situations:

■ **After receiving information, advice, or a referral from a contact:** You should always express your gratitude in writing to individuals who provide you with job search assistance. Not only is this a nice thing to do, it also is functional for a successful job search. Individuals who feel they are appreciated will most likely remember you and be willing to further assist you with your job search and recommend you to others.

■ **Immediately after interviewing for a job:** Whether it be a telephone or face-to-face interview, always write a nice thank you letter within 12-hours of completing the interview. This letter should express your gratitude for having an opportunity to interview for the job. Be sure to reiterate your interest in the job and stress your possible contributions to the employer's operations. The letter should emphasize some of your major strengths in relationship to the employer's needs. All other things being equal, this letter may give you an "extra edge" over other candidates. It may well prove to be the most effective letter in your entire job search!

■ **Withdrawing from further consideration:**  At some point during the recruitment process, you may decide to withdraw from further consideration. Perhaps you decided to take another job, you're now more satisfied with your present job, or the position no longer interests you. For whatever reason, you should write a short thank you letter in which you withdraw from consideration. Explain in positive terms why you are no longer interested in pursuing an application with the organization. Thank them for their time and consideration.

■ **After receiving a rejection:**  Even if you receive a rejection, it's a good idea to write a thank you letter. How many employers ever receive such a letter from what ostensibly should be a disappointed job seeker? This unique letter is likely to be remembered—which is what you want to accomplish in this situation. Being remembered may result in referrals to other employers or perhaps a job interview and offer at some later date.

■ **After receiving a job offer:**  However well they think they hire, employers still are uncertain about the outcome of their hiring decisions until new employees perform in their organization. Why not put their initial anxieties to ease and get off on the right foot by writing a nice thank you letter? In this letter express your appreciation for having received the confidence and trust of the employer. Reiterate what you told the employer during the job interview(s) about your goals and expected performance. Conclude with a reaffirmation of your starting date as well as a statement about how much you look forward to becoming a productive member of the team. Such a thoughtful letter will be well received by the employer. It could well accelerate your progress within the organization beyond the norm.

■ **Upon leaving a job:**  Whether you leave your job voluntarily or are forced by circumstances to terminate, try to leave a positive part of you behind by writing a thank you letter. Burning bridges behind you through face-to-face confrontation or a vindictive, get-even letter may later catch up with you, especially if you anger someone in the process who may later be in a position to affect your career. If you quit to take a job with another organization, thank your employer for the time you spent with the organization and the opportunities given to you to acquire valuable experience and skills. If you terminated under difficult circumstances—organizational cutbacks or a nasty firing—try to leave on as positive a note as possible. Employers in such situations would rather have you out of sight and mind. Assure them there are no hard feelings, and you wish them the best as you would hope they would wish you the same. Stress the positives of your relationship with both the employer and the organization. Remember, your future employer may call your previous employer for information on your past performance. If you leave a stressful situation on a positive note, chances are your previous employer will give you the benefit of the doubt and stress only your positives to others. He may even commit a few "sins of omission" that only you and he know about: *"She really worked well with her co-workers and was one of our best analysts"* does not tell the whole story which may be that you couldn't get along with your boss, and vice versa. After having made peace with each other through the medium of the thank you letter, what would your former employer have to gain by telling the whole story to others about your work with him? Your thank you letter should at least neutralize the situation and at best turn a negative situation into a positive for your career. Indeed, he

may well become one of your supporters—for other jobs with other employers, that is!

The remainder of this chapter presents examples of each type of letter, written according to our principles of effective thank you letters.

Thank you letters should always be written in a timely manner. Make it a practice to sit down and write these letters within 12-hours of the situation that prompts this letter. It should be mailed immediately so that it reaches the recipient within three to four days. If you wait longer, the letter will have less impact on the situation. Indeed, in the case of the interview thank you letter, if an employer is making a final hiring decision among three candidates, your letter should arrive as soon as possible to have a chance to affect the outcome.

Whether you handwrite or type this letter may not make a great deal of difference in terms of outcomes, but your choice says something about your professional style and mentality. Many people claim handwritten thank you letters are more powerful than typed letters. We doubt such claims and have yet to see any credible data on the subject other than personal preferences and questionable logic. It is true that handwritten thank you letters communicate a certain personal element that cannot be expressed in typewritten letters. If you choose to handwrite this letter, make sure you have attractive handwriting. Your handwriting form and style could be a negative.

The problem with handwritten letters is that they can express a certain nonprofessional, amateurish style. They also may raise questions about your motivations and manipulative style. They turn off some readers who expect a business letter, rather than an expression of social graces, in reference to a business situation. Furthermore, some readers may consider the handwritten letter an attempt at psychological manipulation—they know what you're trying to do by handwriting a letter. That's what real estate and car salespeople are taught to do in their training seminars! When in doubt, it's best to type this letter in a neat, clean, and professional manner. If typewritten, such a personal letter also will express your professional style and respond to the expectations appropriate for the situation. It tells the reader that you know proper business etiquette, you know this is a business situation, you are equipped to respond, and you attempt to demonstrate your best professional effort.

## Post Informational Interview

9910 Thompson Drive
Cleveland, OH 43382

June 21, 19____

Jane Evans, Director
EVANS FINANCE CORPORATION
2122 Forman Street
Cleveland, OH 43380

Dear Ms. Evans:

Your advice was most helpful in clarifying my questions on careers in finance. I am now reworking my resume and have included many of your thoughtful suggestions. I will send you a copy next week.

Thanks so much for taking time from your busy schedule to see me. I will keep in contact and follow through on your suggestion to see Sarah Cook about opportunities with the Cleveland-Akron Finance Company.

Sincerely,

Daryl Haines

## Post Informational Interview

9855 Little Glen Court
Dallas, TX 75207

July 29, 19___

Ida Stonewall
PACIFIC DESIGN CENTER
7008 Melrose Avenue
Los Angeles, CA 90069

Dear Ms. Stonewall:

Thank you for taking the time to meet with me yesterday. I thoroughly enjoyed our meeting and the information you gave me was most helpful.

I have already contacted three of the people you suggested I should talk with and have appointments to meet with them over the next two weeks. The fourth person, Jerrie Forsythe, is on vacation so I will try to contact her again next week.

I would appreciate it if you would keep me in mind if you talk with someone in the near future who is looking for an individual with credentials similar to mine. Talking with you only made me more anxious to get into a job in a design center.

As you suggested, I will keep in touch with you over the next few weeks and let you know how my job search is going.

Most sincerely,


JoAnne McGrosney

## Post Informational Interview

4183 Waupelani Drive
State College, PA 16808

December 1, 19___

Dr. Harold Selnik
Chairman
Department of Speech Communication
UNIVERSITY OF PITTSBURGH
Pittsburgh, PA 12511

Dear Dr. Selnik:

Thank you for taking the time to meet with me last Friday. It was most kind of you—especially since you took time from your Thanksgiving break at the university to do so. I found the meeting even more helpful to me than I had anticipated. I had never even considered some of the options open to someone with my major!

I have taken your advice and have made appointments to talk with some of the people whom you suggested. I am sure their advice will also be useful to me.

I will keep in touch with you and let you know what decisions I make and what opportunities I take during the remainder of this year.

Thanks again for helping me make some decisions very important to my future.

Sincerely,

Julie McGuire

## Post Informational Interview

921 West Fifth Street
Denver, CO 72105

July 18, 19_____

James R. Taylor
Assistant Manager
ASSOCIATED FINANCIAL ADVISORS
241 Skyline Road
Denver, CO 71088

Dear Mr. Taylor:

Joan Karvin was right when she said you would be most helpful in advising me on a career in finance.

I appreciated your taking time from your busy schedule to meet with me. Your advice was most helpful and I have incorporated your suggestions into my resume. I will send you a copy next week.

Again, thanks so much for your assistance. As you suggested, I will contact Mr. David James next week in regards to a possible opening with his company.

Sincerely,

John Perkins

## Post Informational Interview

4563 Southshore Drive
Key Biscayne, FL 33455

May 5, 19___

Marlo Sikes
Public Relations Director
DOLPHIN CRUISE LINE
873 North American Way
Miami, FL 33132

Dear Ms. Sikes:

I am grateful for the opportunity to meet with you today. As Mr. Barnes had indicated, you are certainly one of the best informed persons in the Miami area when it comes to questions about the cruise industry. Your knowledge as well as analysis of future trends is right on the mark, yet I had not looked at it that way before.

My discussion with you helped me focus on the direction I want to pursue. I really believe I would be happier working in a cruiseline's corporate offices rather than taking a job on board ship. You mentioned during our discussion that you would be happy to put me in contact with several people in your network if I decided this was the direction I wished to take.

I am writing to ask your assistance in making contact with these people. I will call you in a few days to get these names and addresses from you. I certainly appreciate this additional assistance on your part.

Thank you again for taking time from your busy schedule to meet with me. I look forward to seeing you again in the future—hopefully when I am working for a cruiseline!

Sincerely,

Miriam Jordan

## Post Job Interview

2962 Forrest Drive
Denver, CO 82171

May 28, 19____

Thomas F. Harris
Director, Personnel Department
COASTAL PRODUCTS, INC.
7229 Lakewood Drive
Denver, CO 82170

Dear Mr. Harris:

Thank you again for the opportunity to interview for the marketing position. I appreciated your hospitality and enjoyed meeting you and members of your staff.

The interview convinced me of how compatible my background, interests, and skills are with the goals of Coastal Products Incorporated. My prior marketing experience with the Department of Commerce has prepared me to take a major role in developing both domestic and international marketing strategies. I am confident my work could result in increased market shares for Coastal Products Incorporated in the rapidly expanding Pacific Rim market.

For more information on the new product promotion program I mentioned, call David Garrett at the Department of Commerce; his number is 202/726-0132. I talked to Dave this morning and mentioned your interest in this program.

I look forward to meeting you and your staff again.

Sincerely,

Stephanie Potter

## Post Job Interview

1947 Grace Avenue
Springfield, MA 01281

November 17, _____

James R. Quinn, Director
Personnel Department
DAVIS ENTERPRISES
2290 Cambridge Street
Boston, MA 01181

Dear Mr. Quinn:

Thank you for the opportunity to interview yesterday for the Sales Trainee position. I enjoyed meeting you and learning more about Davis Enterprises. You have a fine staff and a sophisticated approach to marketing.

Your organization appears to be growing in a direction which parallels my interests and career goals. The interview with you and your staff confirmed my initial positive impressions of Davis Enterprises, and I want to reiterate my strong interest in working for you. My prior experience in operating office equipment plus my training in communication would enable me to progress steadily through your training program and become a productive member of your sales team.

Again, thank you for your consideration. If you need any additional information from me, please feel free to call.

Yours truly,

Gail S. Topper

## Post Job Interview

8712 Graham Blvd.
Staunton, VA 23212

January 28, 19___

Edward Jason
Personnel Administrator
CITY OF CHARLESTON
P.O. Box 4561
Charleston, WV 25331

Dear Mr. Jason:

I appreciated the opportunity to interview with you today. Having talked with you and found out in greater depth about the opening you have, I am more sure than ever that I would like to work for the City of Charleston as Parks and Recreation Director.

Having directed all phases of community recreational programs while I was the director in Staunton, I feel certain I could bring the kind of leadership to the program in Charleston that you indicate you need. I also feel certain that under my supervision it would be possible to expand the programs without the need to increase the budget. In these recessionary times that becomes a critical consideration.

I hope to have the opportunity to help Charleston revitalize its recreational programs. Please let me know if I may provide any further information that will be helpful as you make your hiring decision.

I will call you next Friday, as you suggested, to see how your selection process is going.

Sincerely,

Sylvia Whitehurst

## Post Job Interview

882 Forest Lane
Cleveland, OH 43210

March 16, 19____

Jonathan Morrison
Circulation Department
CLEVELAND PLAIN DEALER
8250 Lakefront Blvd.
Cleveland, OH 43208

Dear Mr. Morrison:

I really appreciated having the opportunity to interview with you today for the position of Dispatcher. I remain extremely interested in this position. I am especially interested because it is an evening job. I am used to working an evening schedule and feel I might have trouble adapting to a day job.

If I have not heard from you by next Friday, I will check back with you to see how your selection process is progressing. I look forward to hearing from you and hope I will have the opportunity to work with you.

Sincerely,

Jack Diamond

# Post Job Interview

5680 Citrine Blvd.
Pekin, IL 61559

March 12, 19___

John Dingle
General Manager
PEORIA GAZETTE
13 Walsh Street
Peoria, IL 61564

Dear Mr. Dingle:

I wish to thank you for taking the time to meet with me yesterday. I enjoyed talking with you and finding out more about what is happening at the <u>Peoria Gazette</u>.

I found it fascinating that you are planning to innovate in areas similar to those where we at the <u>Times</u> have made recent changes. I believe I have a lot to offer to the <u>Gazette</u> and ask that you seriously consider me if you decide to restructure and add the new position in Personnel that we talked about. I met several interesting people at lunch with you yesterday and I know I would enjoy working with you and your staff.

I enclose the resume I promised to send you. I will call you in a few days to see whether you have any further questions.

Sincerely,

Jack Fielding

# Referral

5491 Mountain View Dr.
Sacramento, CA 95421

July 28, 19___

Martha Albertson
Personnel Department
HOLIDAY INN NATIONAL
319 Granite Stone Dr.
San Diego, CA 92351

Dear Ms. Albertson:

Sorry my letter in response to your ad in the San Diego Times arrived too late for me to be considered for the position. It certainly was kind of you to take time to suggest that I contact Dorothy Wiggins of Inn Tonight.

I have talked with Miss Wiggins and although she does not have an opening I might fit at present, she indicated if I would send her a resume she would keep it on file.

I am writing to ask that you do the same. I am still very much interested in Holiday Inn National and hope that you will consider me for the next opening you may have. I enclose an additional copy of my resume for your information. My broad experience in guest services management would make me an ideal addition to your team.

I will hope to hear from you and will be in touch with you the next time I am in San Diego in about a month.

Sincerely,


Arthur Brenner

# Referral

485 High Bluff Road
Santa Fe, NM 89543

November 16, 19___

Rebecca Lyons
WESTERN INDUSTRIES, INC.
98347 W. Main Street
Albuquerque, NM 89977

Dear Mrs. Lyons:

I want to thank you for the referral you gave me. At your suggestion I contacted Deborah Johnson at Southwestern Products. The timing was perfect. They had an opening, I was interviewed and offered the job. I will be starting there next week!

The job will be a promotion of sorts for me as well, since I will be the executive secretary to the vice-president of operations. I look forward to my work there.

Sincerely,

Karen Jostney

## Referral

9821 West Fulton Street
Miami, FL 30303

March 7, 19____

Martin Davis
213 Doreen Drive
Miami, FL 30301

Dear Martin,

Thanks so much for putting me in contact with Jane Burton at Fordham Manufacturing Company.

I spoke with her today about my interests in technical training. She was most gracious with her time and provided me with a great deal of useful information on job opportunities in the Miami area. She even made some valuable suggestions for strengthening my resume and gave me a few names of individuals who might be interested in my qualifications.

I'll send you a copy of my resume once I revise it. Please feel free to make any comments or suggestions as well as share it with others who might be interested in my background.

Again, thanks so much for putting me in contact with Jane Burton. She spoke very highly of you and your work with the United Fund.

Sincerely,

Steven Zolbert

# Responding to Rejection

1947 Grace Avenue
Springfield, MA 01281

September 14, 19____

Sharon T. Avery
Vice President for Sales
BENTLEY ENTERPRISES
529 W. Sheridan Road
Washington, DC 20011

Dear Ms. Avery:

Thank you for giving me the opportunity to interview for the Customer Services Representative position. I appreciate your consideration and interest in me. I learned a great deal from our meetings.

Although I am disappointed in not being selected for your current vacancy, I want you to know that I appreciated the courtesy and professionalism shown to me during the entire selection process. I enjoyed meeting you, John Roberts, and other members of your sales staff. My meetings confirmed that Bentley Enterprises would be an exciting place to work and build a career.

I want to reiterate my strong interest in working for you. Please keep me in mind should another position become available in the near future.

Again, thank you for the opportunity to interview. Best wishes to you and your staff.

Yours truly,

Gail S. Topper

# Responding to Rejection

455 Los Altos Drive
Los Angeles, CA 91095

October 24, 19___

Jennifer Strong
THE GREEN BEAN CO.
241 Greenbrier Road
Los Angeles, CA 91093

Dear Mrs. Strong:

I was sorry to hear of the selection of another candidate to fill the slot of manager of the first of three stores you will be opening in the L.A. area. However, I am certain that you had good reasons for the choice you made. My disappointment at not having been selected is someone else's joy.

I know you plan to open two more stores in this area over the next few months. I am writing to request that you keep my resume in an "open" file and reconsider my application for the two other slots as they become available. In fact, I enclose an additional copy of my resume for your convenience.

I have a high regard for your products, think my experience could serve you well and hope to have the opportunity to talk with you again regarding future openings you will have in the L.A. area.

Thank you for your consideration.

Sincerely,

Linda Perry

## Withdrawing From Consideration

4458 Enfield Drive
Norfolk, VA 23506

September 30, 19___

Jeffrey Allen
JEFFERSON MORTGAGE COMPANY
1873 Granby Street
Norfolk, VA 23500

Dear Mr. Allen:

On September 16th, I sent a cover letter and resume to you in response to your advertisement for a loan officer. Since I have not heard from you, I do not know whether my application is presently under consideration.

However, since I have just accepted a position with the Bank of Commerce, I am writing to request that you withdraw my application from consideration.

I have a high regard for your institution that has remained financially strong as a result of conservative lending practices. Perhaps our paths will cross and we will have the opportunity to meet in the future.

Sincerely,

Wanda Wright

## Withdrawing From Consideration

3773 Nevada Street
Portland, OR 98677

July 5, 19___

Ann Jenkins
KALIN'S DRESS SHOP
3456 Centre Street
Portland, OR 98678

Dear Mrs. Jenkins:

Thank you for giving me the opportunity to talk with you yesterday about the opening you have for a salesperson at your store.

You were more helpful than you know. I had always thought working in a dress shop would be fun—the chance to work with all those pretty clothes! After talking with you, I realize how much hard work is involved before the clothing makes its way to the racks in the store. I no longer believe this is the right line of work for me. Thank you for helping me make an important decision.

You have a beautiful store and I have no doubt you will have no difficulty finding the right person to fill your sales opening.

Sincerely,

Angelique Martin

## Withdrawing From Consideration

2345 Glen Echo Court
Berea, OH 44375

October 7, 19___

Dr. Harriet Learner
Chair
Department of Communication
CUYAHOGA COMMUNITY COLLEGE
Cleveland, OH 44452

Dear Dr. Learner:

Thank you for selecting me to interview for the instructor position open in the Communication Department for the coming academic year. I appreciated the opportunity to meet with you and other members of the faculty. You have an outstanding program and it would be a privilege for me to have the opportunity to work with you.

However, I must request that you withdraw my application from further consideration. I have just received an offer from the Leeward Community College in Pearl City, Hawaii, to teach in their Department of Speech Communication. This position will give me the chance to further my study of the linguistic components of Native American speech; I hope to be able to complete the book I am writing within the year.

I know you will have no trouble selecting a competent candidate to fill your opening. I do plan to return to Ohio within a year or two to be closer to my parents, and I hope we may be able to get together again at that time. If you have an opening next year in my areas of specialty, I would very much appreciate hearing about it at that time.

I will keep in touch with you over the next year.

Sincerely,

Marcus McDonald

## Withdrawing From Consideration

733 Main Street
Williamsburg, VA 23512

December 1, 19___

Dr. Thomas C. Bostelli, President
NORTHERN STATES UNIVERSITY
2500 University Drive
Greenfield, MA 03241

Dear Dr. Bostelli:

It was indeed a pleasure meeting with you and your staff last week to discuss your need for a Director of Public and Government Relations. Our time together was most enjoyable and informative.

As I discussed with you during our meetings, I believe one purpose of preliminary interviews is to explore areas of mutual interest and to assess the fit between the individual and the position. After careful consideration, I have decided to withdraw from consideration for the position.

My decision is based upon several factors. First, the emphasis on fund raising is certainly needed, but I would prefer more balance in my work activities. Second, the position would require more travel than I am willing to accept with my other responsibilities. Third, professional opportunities for my husband would be very limited in northwest Massachusetts.

I want to thank you for interviewing me and giving me the opportunity to learn about your needs. You have a fine staff and faculty, and I would have enjoyed working with them.

Best wishes in your search.

Sincerely,

Janet L. Lawson

# Accepting Job Offer

2589 Jason Drive
Ithaca, NY 14850

August 19, 19____

Sharon A. Waters
Personnel Director
NEW YORK STATE POLICE
Administrative Division
892 South Park
Albany, NY 11081

Dear Ms. Waters:

I want to thank you and Mr. Gordon for giving me the opportunity to work with the New York State Police. I am very pleased to accept the position as a research and data analyst with your planning unit. The position requires exactly the kind of work I want to do, and I know that I will do a good job for you.

As we discussed, I shall begin work on October 1. In the meantime, I shall compete all the necessary employment forms, obtain the required physical examination, and locate housing. I plan to be in Albany within the next two weeks and would like to deliver the paperwork to you personally. At that time we could handle any remaining items pertaining to my employment. I'll call next week to schedule an appointment with you.

I enjoyed my interviews with you and Mr. Gordon and look forward to beginning my job with the Planning Unit.

Sincerely,

Cheryl Ayers

cc: Mr. Edward Gordon, Administrator
    Planning Unit

## Accepting Job Offer

8172 Western Avenue
Cedar Rapids, IA 54019

September 29, 19____

Morris Edelson
ICRW INTERNATIONAL
28 W. 32nd Street
New York, NY 10031

Dear Mr. Edelson:

I was so pleased to receive the job offer from ICRW. I am appreciative of the confidence you have in my work and I will work hard to deserve the support you are giving me. I don't know which I am more excited about—the work I will be doing or the location where I will be working. The chance to work on-site in Indonesia will be extremely interesting.

I look forward to working with you and the staff of ICRW over the coming year.

Sincerely,

Lynne Gardner

## Accepting Job Offer

712 W. Vermont St.
Washington, DC 20132

June 10, 19___

Elliott Stevens
WASHINGTON MONTHLY
1611 Connecticut Ave., NW
Washington, DC 20009

Dear Mr. Stevens:

It is with great anticipation that I accept your offer of a summer internship with the Washington Monthly. I appreciate the confidence that you obviously have in me and promise that I will not disappoint you. I am sure my work with you will help me with my journalism studies when I return to school in the fall.

I will plan to begin work on the June 21, as we discussed. Please let me know if there is any paperwork I need to complete before reporting to work that day.

Sincerely,

Tracey Nelson

## Accepting Job Offer

7694 James Courts
San Francisco, CA 94826

June 7, 19____

Judith Greene
Vice President
WEST COAST AIRLINES
2400 Van Ness
San Francisco, CA 94829

Dear Ms. Greene:

I am pleased to accept your offer, and I am looking forward to joining you and your staff next month.

The customer relations position is ideally suited to my background and interests. I assure you I will give you my best effort in making this an effective position within your company.

I understand I will begin work on July 1. If, in the meantime, I need to complete any paper work or take care of any other matters, please contact me at 377-4029.

I enjoyed meeting with you and your staff and appreciated the professional manner in which the hiring was conducted.

Sincerely,

Joan Kitner

## Responding to Rejection

781 Humphrey Blvd.
Minneapolis, MN 53821

August 22, 19___

Sandra Delray
OLLEN GRAPHICS
182 Thompson Ave.
Suite 914
Minneapolis, MN 53824

Dear Ms. Delray:

I have just received your letter indicating that another candidate was selected for the position I interviewed for—a graphic artist. Of course I am disappointed, but I am sure you will be pleased with the person you selected.

I wish to take this opportunity to thank you for your consideration. I really appreciated the professional way in which the hiring process was conducted. I enjoyed meeting many of the artists in your firm and believe I would have worked well with them.

Please keep me in mind when you have another opening in your firm. I remain very interested in your company and the fine work you do.

Sincerely,

Debra Summers

## Responding to Rejection

179 W. 27th Street
San Francisco, CA 94131

October 3, 19____

Betsy Kramer
AMERICAN SCHOOL BOARDS
  ASSOCIATION
2792 Hillcrest Dr.
San Francisco, CA 94123

Dear Ms. Kramer:

I received your letter today, indicating that you had made a hiring decision. I regret that I was not the individual selected for the position, but I appreciate your letting me know of your decision in such a timely manner. I also appreciate the professional manner in which all aspects of the hiring process were conducted.

Please keep my resume on file. In fact, I am enclosing an additional copy for you in the event that the one I submitted earlier will be filed with other applications for the position you have already filled. I really believe my skills would be useful to your association and I know I would enjoy working with your staff. I would appreciate hearing from you if you should have a similar opening in the near future.

Thank you again for your consideration.

Sincerely,

Julie Stroomer

## Terminating Employment

6336 Boulder Avenue
Denver, CO 80976

July 31, 19____

Gerald Mockitis
General Manager
DENVER SUN TIMES
80796 County Line Road
Denver, CO 80911

Dear Mr. Mockitis:

When I accepted my position three years ago, I discussed with you my plans to return to graduate school within 3-5 years. I have decided that this is the best time for me to make this move, and hence I will be resigning my position effective September 1st.

I want to thank you for the opportunity to work for the Sun Times. I have learned a great deal about personnel administration and my experiences here have helped me to better focus on my goals for graduate school.

I will miss all my colleagues at the Sun Times and hope to be able to keep in touch with you over the next year.

Sincerely,

Alfred Merrill

## Terminating Employment

1099 Seventh Avenue
Akron, OH 44522

August 2, 19____


James T. Thomas
Chief Engineer
AKRON CONSTRUCTION COMPANY
1170 South Hills Highway
Akron, OH 44524


Dear Jim,

I am writing to inform you that I will be leaving Akron Construction Company on September 12 to accept another position.

As you know, I have developed an interest in architectural drafting which combines my drafting skills with my artistic interests. While I was vacationing in Houston recently, a relative approached me about an opening for someone with my background with a large architecture and engineering firm. I investigated the possibility and subsequently received an offer. After careful consideration, I decided to accept the offer and relocate to Houston. I will be working with Brown and Little Company.

I have thoroughly enjoyed working with you over the past two years, and deeply appreciate your fine supervision and support. You have taught me a great deal about drafting, and I want to thank you for providing me with the opportunity to work here. It has been a very positive experience for me both personally and professionally.

I wanted to give you more than the customary two weeks notice so you would have time to find my replacement. I made the decision to relocate yesterday and decided to inform you immediately.

Best wishes.


Sincerely,


John Albert

# Chapter Eleven

# SPECIAL AND UNUSUAL LETTERS

---

Most letters presented in this book are conventional job search letters aimed at audiences that expect to receive such letters. Our examples present job seekers as enthusiastic, intelligent, capable, likable, and action-oriented—personal and professional characteristics sought by employers in candidates.

Our final set of letters goes beyond the conventional. Not expecting to receive such communication from job seekers, employers react to unconventional letters in different ways. Some are sufficiently impressed by the writer's creativity, entrepreneurialism, and drive that the employer remembers, interviews, and hires the candidate. Other employers are turned off by the aggressive and sometimes silly

nature of such communication. Whatever the reaction, for better or for worse, these forms of communication do impress readers.

We caution you about writing unconventional job search communication. They elicit different responses from different audiences. If, for example, you are applying for an artistic or sales position, you may want to demonstrate your creativity or entrepreneurialism in your written communication. For the graphic artist, this might take the form of a special graphic incorporated in a letter. For someone in the print media, this could involve a headlined newspaper article about the individual reporting a story or a press release announcing an exceptional performer. For the salesperson, the classic letter accompanying the shoe-in-the-box has worked for some individuals who literally demonstrate their entrepreneurial nature by approaching strangers in such an unconventional manner. Many employers may feel such an approach may translate into new sales and clients.

Be your own judge as to the appropriateness of such unconventional communication. Keep in mind your audience. If, for example, you are applying for a position in banking, law, government, or education, remember the hiring cultures of these occupations tend to be conservative. On the other hand, the unconventional job search letter, memo, telegram, or card can sufficiently impress an employer to call you for an interview.

Whatever you do, know that in a job search there is no guarantee that anything works for every situation. How you choose to communicate—both message and medium—will tell the potential employer about how you will work with them.

## Press Release
(Broadcast)

---

**AUTOMOTIVE/**                                **FOR IMMEDIATE RELEASE**
**WAREHOUSE NEWS**                                  Tel. 919/738-2981

---

### INNOVATIVE WAREHOUSE INVENTORY SYSTEM
### REDUCES LABOR COSTS BY 35%!

Yes, it's true. A newly installed inventory system reduced labor costs by 35% at J. L. Automotive Parts. Mark Timpson, an employee with over seven years experience in parts management, developed an innovative inventory system custom-designed to meet the growing demand for used antique car parts. "It really wasn't as difficult as I thought," Mark explains. "I worked with a fine team of professionals who really know the parts business. We put our heads together over a three week period to create a new computerized system that reduced our labor costs by 35% within eight months."

For his team efforts, Mark received the Employee of the Year award. He believes this system is easily adapted to other automotive parts businesses and warehouse operations. He's prepared to demonstrate this approach to parties interested in strengthening their warehouse management systems.

#       #       #

For further information, including a detailed resume, or for scheduling an interview or demonstration, contact:

Mark Timpson
1873 Tyson Road
San Diego, CA 98712
Tel. 919/738-2981

## Shoe-in-the-Box
(resume inserted in shoe)

**ANGEL ROBERTS**

819 Collier Drive ▪ San Jose, CA 94011 ▪ 917/371-9021

July 19, 19____

Milton Whitehead
Director of Sales
SATURN PHARMACEUTICAL CO.
7213 American Drive
St. Louis, MO 63811

Dear Mr. Whitehead:

Now that I have my shoe in the door, how about an interview?

Expecting a call,

Angel Roberts

## Telegram

RESUME ARRIVING TOMORROW NOON BY FEDERAL EX-
PRESS. PLEASE EXAMINE CAREFULLY. CANDIDATE (SHEILA
WATSON) WITH THREE YEARS EXPERIENCE DEVELOPING
HIGHLY SUCCESSFUL ART LEASING PROGRAM WISHES TO
INTERVIEW FOR RECENTLY ADVERTISED LEASING MANAG-
ER POSITION. ENCLOSING SAMPLE BROCHURES AND
STRATEGIC MARKETING PLAN FOR YOUR REVIEW. EXPECT-
ING EXCELLENT MARKET IN SECOND HALF OF YEAR BASED
ON RECENT ANALYSIS OF CORPORATE ART ACQUISITION
PATTERNS. WILLING TO TRAVEL AND RELOCATE. CALL
317/378-9871 OR FAX 317/378-8712 FOR MORE INFORMATION
OR APPOINTMENT.

## 3 x 5 Announcement Card

**WHERE DO YOU FIND
FRESH TALENT FOR
PROMOTING RENEWABLE
ENERGY ISSUES?**

I may just be out of college, but I
have something most other college
graduates lack—three years of environmental activism at both the state
and local level.

You'll find my resume on the back of
this card. Let's talk soon. I think we
could work well together on issues we
both are committed to seeing translated into public policy.

Contact:  Janet Trueblood
          Tel. 216/332-3829

# CAREER RESOURCES

Call or write Impact Publications to receive a free copy of their latest comprehensive and annotated catalog of over 1,000 career resources (books, subscriptions, training programs, videos, audiocassettes, computer software).

The following career resources are available directly from Impact Publications. Complete this form or list the titles, include postage (see formula at the end), enclose payment, specify your name and address, and send your order to:

**IMPACT PUBLICATIONS**
9104-N Manassas Drive
Manassas Park, VA 22111
Tel. 703/361-7300
FAX 703/335-9486

Orders from individuals must be prepaid by check, moneyorder, Visa or MasterCard number. We accept telephone and FAX orders with a Visa or MasterCard number.

| Qty. | Titles | Price | TOTAL |
|------|--------|-------|-------|

## LETTERS AND RESUMES

| Qty. | Titles | Price | TOTAL |
|------|--------|-------|-------|
| ____ | 171 High-Impact Cover Letters | $10.95 | ____ |
| ____ | 200 Letters For Job Hunters | 17.95 | ____ |
| ____ | Cover Letters That Knock 'Em Dead | 7.95 | ____ |
| ____ | Damn Good Resume Guide | 6.95 | ____ |
| ____ | Dynamite Cover Letters | 9.95 | ____ |
| ____ | Dynamite Resumes | 9.95 | ____ |
| ____ | Encyclopedia of Job-Winning Resumes | 16.95 | ____ |
| ____ | High Impact Resumes and Letters | 12.95 | ____ |
| ____ | Job Search Letters That Get Results | 12.95 | ____ |
| ____ | Just Resumes | 9.95 | ____ |
| ____ | No-Pain Resume Workbook | 14.95 | ____ |
| ____ | Perfect Cover Letter | 9.95 | ____ |
| ____ | Perfect Resume | 10.95 | ____ |
| ____ | Resume Catalog | 15.95 | ____ |
| ____ | Resume Solution | 10.95 | ____ |
| ____ | Resume Writing | 9.95 | ____ |
| ____ | Resume Writing Made Essay | 9.95 | ____ |
| ____ | Resumes, Resumes, Resumes | 8.95 | ____ |
| ____ | Resumes That Knock 'Em Dead | 7.95 | ____ |
| ____ | Revising Your Resume | 13.95 | ____ |
| ____ | Sure-Hire Resumes | 14.95 | ____ |
| ____ | Your First Resume | 10.95 | ____ |

## COMPUTER SOFTWARE (all IBM; some Apple available)

| | |
|---|---|
| ___ Creative Resume | 139.95 ___ |
| ___ INSTANT™ Job Winning Letters System | 39.95 ___ |
| ___ JOBHUNT™ Quick & Easy Employer Contacts | 49.95 ___ |
| ___ LETTERWORKS™: 400 Letters, Memos, Press Releases, etc. | 79.95 ___ |
| ___ Perfect Resume Computer Kit (Personal) | 49.95 ___ |
| ___ Quick & Easy 171's (Individual) | 49.95 ___ |
| ___ ResumeMaker™ | 49.95 ___ |
| ___ Right Resume Writer I | 59.95 ___ |
| ___ Right Resume Writer II | 102.95 ___ |
| ___ Right Resume Writer III | 102.95 ___ |

## RESUME VIDEOS

| | |
|---|---|
| ___ Does Your Resumes Wear Blue Jeans? Resume Writing Workshop | 129.95 ___ |
| ___ The Miracle Resume | 99.95 ___ |
| ___ Video Resume Writer | 102.95 ___ |

## JOB SEARCH STRATEGIES AND TACTICS

| | |
|---|---|
| ___ Careering and Re-Careering For the 1990s | 13.95 ___ |
| ___ Complete Job Search Handbook | 12.95 ___ |
| ___ Discover the Best Jobs For You | 11.95 ___ |
| ___ Guerrilla Tactics in the New Job Market | 11.95 ___ |
| ___ Super Job Search | 22.95 ___ |
| ___ What Color Is Your Parachute? | 12.95 ___ |

## ALTERNATIVE JOBS, CAREERS, AND EMPLOYERS

| | |
|---|---|
| ___ 101 Careers | 12.95 ___ |
| ___ America's 50 Fastest Growing Jobs | 9.95 ___ |
| ___ American Almanac of Jobs and Salaries | 15.95 ___ |
| ___ Best Jobs For the 1990s and Into the 21st Century | 12.95 ___ |
| ___ Career Finder | 14.95 ___ |
| ___ Dictionary of Occupational Titles (1991 ed.) | 39.95 ___ |
| ___ Directory of Executive Recruiters (annual) | 39.95 ___ |
| ___ Directory of Outplacement Firms (annual) | 69.95 ___ |
| ___ Educator's Guide To Alternative Jobs and Careers | 13.95 ___ |
| ___ Encyclopedia of Careers and Vocational Guidance | 129.95 ___ |
| ___ Environmental Career Guide | 14.95 ___ |
| ___ Flying High in Travel | 16.95 ___ |
| ___ Job Opportunities For Business & Liberal Arts Jobs | 20.95 ___ |
| ___ Job Opportunities For Engineering, Science, & Computer Graduates | 20.95 ___ |
| ___ Jobs! What They Are, Where They Are... | 14.95 ___ |
| ___ Jobs 1992 | 15.95 ___ |
| ___ Jobs For People Who Love Travel | 12.95 ___ |
| ___ Jobs Rated Almanac | 16.95 ___ |
| ___ New Emerging Careers | 14.95 ___ |
| ___ Occupational Outlook Handbook (biannual) | 21.95 ___ |
| ___ Professional's Job Finder | 15.95 ___ |
| ___ Where the Jobs Are | 15.95 ___ |

## SELF-ASSESSMENT AND GOAL SETTING

| | |
|---|---|
| ___ Discover What You're Best At | 10.95 ___ |
| ___ New Quick Job Hunting Map | 3.95 ___ |

| | | |
|---|---|---|
| ____ Three Boxes of Life | 14.95 | ____ |
| ____ Truth About You | 11.95 | ____ |
| ____ Where Do I Go From Here With My Life? | 11.95 | ____ |
| ____ Wishcraft | 9.95 | ____ |

## SELF-ESTEEM, PROBLEM SOLVING, MANAGING CHANGE

| | | |
|---|---|---|
| ____ Bouncing Back | 14.95 | ____ |
| ____ Celebrate Yourself | 9.95 | ____ |
| ____ Do What You Love, and the Money Will Follow | 8.95 | ____ |
| ____ Fortysomething | 18.95 | ____ |
| ____ Getting Unstuck | 9.95 | ____ |
| ____ Work With Passion | 9.95 | ____ |

## INTERVIEWS, NETWORKING, AND SALARIES

| | | |
|---|---|---|
| ____ Dynamite Answers To Interview Questions | 9.95 | ____ |
| ____ Great Connections: Small Talk & Networking For Businesspeople | 11.95 | ____ |
| ____ How To Get Interviews From Job Ads | 16.95 | ____ |
| ____ Interview For Success | 11.95 | ____ |
| ____ Listening: The Forgotten Skill | 12.95 | ____ |
| ____ Knock 'Em Dead With Great Answers To Interview Questions | 19.95 | ____ |
| ____ Network Your Way To Job and Career Success | 11.95 | ____ |
| ____ Perfect Follow-up to Win the Job | 9.95 | ____ |
| ____ Power Networking | 14.95 | ____ |
| ____ Salary Success | 11.95 | ____ |
| ____ Sweaty Palms | 9.95 | ____ |

## DRESS, APPEARANCE, AND IMAGE

| | | |
|---|---|---|
| ____ Dress For Success | 10.95 | ____ |
| ____ How To Present a Professional Image Video (2 tapes) | 149.95 | ____ |
| ____ Miss Manners' Guide To the Turn of the Millennium | 24.95 | ____ |
| ____ Professional Image | 10.95 | ____ |
| ____ Professional Presence | 21.95 | ____ |
| ____ Secret Language of Success | 10.95 | ____ |
| ____ Women's Dress For Success | 8.95 | ____ |

## PUBLIC-ORIENTED CAREERS

| | | |
|---|---|---|
| ____ 171 Reference Book | 18.95 | ____ |
| ____ Almanac of American Government Jobs and Careers | 14.95 | ____ |
| ____ Book of American Government Jobs | 15.95 | ____ |
| ____ Complete Guide To Public Employment | 15.95 | ____ |
| ____ Find a Federal Job Fast! | 9.95 | ____ |
| ____ Good Works | 18.00 | ____ |
| ____ Government Job Finder | 14.95 | ____ |
| ____ How To Get a Federal Job | 15.00 | ____ |
| ____ Jobs and Careers With Nonprofit Organizations | 13.95 | ____ |
| ____ Non-Profits' Job Finder | 13.95 | ____ |
| ____ Profitable Careers In Nonprofits | 14.95 | ____ |

## INTERNATIONAL AND OVERSEAS JOBS

| | | |
|---|---|---|
| ____ Almanac of International Jobs and Careers | 14.95 | ____ |
| ____ Complete Guide To International Jobs and Careers | 13.95 | ____ |
| ____ How To Get a Job In Europe | 15.95 | ____ |

| | | |
|---|---|---|
| ____ How To Get a Job In the Pacific Rim | 17.95 | ____ |
| ____ International Careers | 10.95 | ____ |
| ____ International Jobs | 12.95 | ____ |
| ____ Passport To Overseas Employment | 14.95 | ____ |
| ____ Teaching English Abroad | 13.95 | ____ |
| ____ Work Your Way Around the World | 16.95 | ____ |
| ____ Work, Study, Travel Abroad | 12.95 | ____ |

## MILITARY AND SPOUSES

| | | |
|---|---|---|
| ____ Beyond the Uniform | 12.95 | ____ |
| ____ Does Your Resume Wear Combat Boots? | 7.95 | ____ |
| ____ Job Search: Marketing Your Military Experience | 14.95 | ____ |
| ____ Re-Entry | 13.95 | ____ |
| ____ Relocating Spouse's Guide To Employment | 12.95 | ____ |
| ____ Retiring From the Military | 22.95 | ____ |
| ____ Today's Military Wife | 14.95 | ____ |

## STUDENTS AND RECENT GRADUATES

| | | |
|---|---|---|
| ____ College Majors and Careers | 15.95 | ____ |
| ____ Graduating To the 9-5 World | 11.95 | ____ |
| ____ How You Really Get Hired | 8.95 | ____ |
| ____ Liberal Arts Jobs | 10.95 | ____ |
| ____ Major Options | 12.95 | ____ |
| ____ Put Your Degree To Work | 9.95 | ____ |

**SUBTOTAL** ____

Virginia residents add
4½% sales tax ____

**POSTAGE/HANDLING**
($3.00 for first title and 75¢    $3.00
for each additional book) ____

**TOTAL ENCLOSED** ---------------- ____

**NAME** _____

**ADDRESS** _____

_____

**CITY** _____ **STATE** _____ **ZIP** _____

[ ] I enclose check/money order for $ _____ made payable
to IMPACT PUBLICATIONS

[ ] Please charge $ _____ to my credit card:

[ ] Visa    [ ] MasterCard

Card # _____

Expiration date _____/_____

Signature _____